The Essence of
International
Marketing

The Essence of Management Series

Published titles

The Essence of Total Quality Management
The Essence of Strategic Management
The Essence of International Money
The Essence of Management Accounting
The Essence of Financial Accounting
The Essence of Marketing Research
The Essence of Information Systems
The Essence of Successful Staff Selection
The Essence of Effective Communication
The Essence of Statistics for Business
The Essence of Business Taxation
The Essence of the Economy
The Essence of Mathematics for Business
The Essence of Organizational Behaviour
The Essence of Small Business
The Essence of Business Economics
The Essence of Operations Management
The Essence of Services Marketing
The Essence of International Business
The Essence of Marketing

Forthcoming titles

The Essence of Public Relations
The Essence of Managing People
The Essence of Financial Management
The Essence of Change
The Essence of Business Law
The Essence of Women in Management
The Essence of Mergers and Acquisitions
The Essence of Industrial Relations and Personnel Management
The Essence of Influencing Skills
The Essence of Services Management
The Essence of Industrial Marketing
The Essence of Venture Capital and New Ventures

The Essence of International Marketing

Stanley J. Paliwoda
University of Calgary

Prentice Hall

New York   London   Toronto   Sydney   Tokyo   Singapore

First published 1994 by
Prentice Hall International (UK) Ltd
Campus 400, Maylands Avenue
Hemel Hempstead
Hertfordshire, HP2 7EZ
A division of
Simon & Schuster International Group

Typeset in 10/12 pt Palatino
by Keyset Composition, Colchester

Printed and bound in Great Britain by
BPCC Wheatons Ltd, Exeter

Library of Congress Cataloging-in-Publication Data

Paliwoda, Stanley J.
 The essence of international marketing / Stanley J. Paliwoda.
  p.   cm. – (The Essence of management series)
 Includes bibliographical references and index.
 ISBN 0–13–284803–1
  1. Export marketing—Management.   I. Title.   II. Series.
 HF1416.P348 1993
 658.8'48—dc20   93–36374
                                                                         CIP

British Library Cataloguing in Publication Data

A catalogue record for this book is available from
the British Library

ISBN 0-13-284803-1

---

1 2 3 4 5   98 97 96 95 94

Contents

Preface

The Essence series of books is aimed at the experienced practitioner and MBA market. There is little need in this book to construct an elegant academic framework on which to build a superstructure as a more practical framework exists already in the minds of the readers to whom this book and this series as a whole are targeted.

Background detail and explanation are brief so as to concentrate analysis on the main issues at the micro or company level, assessing always the likelihood of change, the implications that change will bring and how best to respond to change. This is by no means a descriptive book. It does not set out to describe in detail what is here today. Instead, it focuses on the pressures that exist today and that will lead to a new tomorrow for both companies and for consumers such as ourselves. Perhaps, then, it is more of a 'rune' than a 'tome'!

In outline, the book is simple to follow, being based around nine Ps, one chapter being devoted to each but also pointing out the interaction that exists between them. For too long those in marketing education have taught that there are only four Ps (product, place, promotion, price) and that all can be solved with the correct magical formulation by the supplier of these four P variables. This may be true of markets where buyers and sellers are passive, but these do not exist any more, if indeed they ever did. Customers today can no longer be dictated to, because they are more product-knowledgeable than at any time in the past and because they are the focus of ever-increasing competitive actions to win them over. This is equally applicable when we consider entire country markets. All of the easy markets are gone. Instead, we have growth limited to markets such as that of China or the former USSR, now fragmented into the Commonwealth of Independent States (CIS) composed of proudly independent republics. Our trading environment in terms of market structure and buyer knowledge, power and expectations has changed materially and so we need new tools to deal with these new market dynamics. Instead of just developing managers, we need to develop managers to become good competitors. In this light, the four Ps is a useless box of tricks for today's markets. This, then, is not a conventional book, for there are enough of them around already. Instead, it sets out to be a 'thinking' book which confronts problems and leads the reader through a series of scenarios and questions so as to challenge managerial thinking. Each chapter concludes with a checklist of what managers need to know, labelled 'Be aware'.

This book is not constructed with a syllabus in mind but rather a need to formulate managerial attention and focus on the key marketing issues related to international marketing. Managers should find this book to be of practical help and relevance. For those seeking a more detailed general textbook, I have provided for that need in *International Marketing*, now in its second edition with Butterworth-Heinemann, Oxford (1993).

In order to be read by managers, this book has to be concise. To be concise, it must in turn be brief, but to succeed it has to be comprehensive in coverage and adequate in explanation. I hope that I have provided just such a book which falls well within this zone of acceptability as perceived by you, the consumer.

Stanley J. Paliwoda, University of Calgary

Introduction

International marketing as a set of skills has increasingly come into focus in the last few years. The world is forever changing, but the events that have taken place since 1989 have been particularly dramatic. There have been border changes, country name changes and even technological innovations in cartography that have altered the traditional depiction of countries in both shape and size. Simultaneously, another trend has been taking place with the formation of trading blocs, whether it be the ever-expanding European Community or the nascent North American Free Trade Agreement. These trading blocs are important in themselves, but within and amongst themselves, member states have been able to reduce, if not eliminate in some cases, many of the traditional barriers to trade. Internally that is something to be welcomed, but for those on the outside it creates fears of possible protectionism and of a 'fortress' mentality.

While this has been happening on the macro level it is also important not to lose sight of the consumer. The individual consumer does not see himself or herself as a global consumer, but is still proud to be a patriot while enjoying the benefits of belonging to a greater economic union. It is one of the paradoxes of the twentieth century that this centrifugal force, which drives more and more towards economic and trading unions, should awaken desires for national independence and sovereignty. It is important that marketers do not lose sight of this highly important development and the potential which it holds for exporters as well as investors.

Marketing has itself changed over time and has undergone

various stages in its evolution, but perhaps the most important tool handed down to us from the marketing literature is that of segmentation, thanks to the information age which has been spawned by computerization. Globally we can exploit consumer needs while we custom-build products for specific groups of individuals. Needs cross frontiers, whether the products in general relate to food, shampoo or sanitary towels. Significantly, marketers have found that practising segmentation means that they are able to access similar groups of consumers to those in their own domestic market with little added cost in necessary product adaptation required by local laws on labelling, packaging, language or use of certain ingredients, colours or flavourings. Computerization allows us to track the consumer to a degree that was not possible ten or fifteen years ago, but today the one who is sitting on this information is not the manufacturer, but the retailer. There has been a significant power shift taking place in that retailers hold vital consumer-buying information in their store credit cards that profiles their consumer. Computerization has also provided the knowledge of consumer-buying patterns per store, so we can now access fuller and much more comprehensive data than at any previous time in commercial history. If we know our customer profile we can then consider how to target this audience and companies such as SRI International, with their VALS (values and lifestyles) segmentation of a society at large, prove useful in helping to determine not just the advertising or promotional message that is required, but also how to reach that target audience and by which form of media.

The global village is coming nearer in that we are now all more easily accessible by communications, but the net effect is that while affluence and world trade remain in the Western hemisphere, there is increasing 'noise' from competitors also eager to push their similar competitive offerings to the same market segments and usually through the same media and distribution channels. Although the youth market and popular music are becoming more and more standardized internationally, these are but two examples that swim against a tide of trade restrictions as well as cultural constraints. In the 1990s there are still few global products in existence. While the IBM PC and McDonald's restaurants begin to join the ranks of Coca-Cola and Pepsi-Cola, it should also be pointed out that both have seen many copycat imitations not just in Western countries, but in Africa, India and the countries of Eastern Europe which have rejected communism to varying degrees. Product counterfeiting has become a problem for the copyright owners and is a major component of world trade. No one will openly admit to counterfeiting taking place with their products, but even in the mid-1980s it was estimated to be 9 per cent of world trade and increasing.

The source of these counterfeit products is mainly the countries in which they are sold and, second, the Pacific Basin countries which have free-port status and thus further tax and custom advantages on top of their lower labour costs. Consumer tastes are fuelled by media that thrive on a product-hungry public for their advertising revenues. Choice and competition force prices down, creating a rationale for 'runaway industry' that seeks to exploit price advantages the world over by continually shifting its productive resources across frontiers.

The knowledgeable, cynical, advertising-hardened Western consumer seeks quality. In manufacturing terms this has given rise to a quest for what has been termed 'low-cost excellence' whereby product quality has to be maintained while achieving all possible cost-saving opportunities. This is a requirement of trading on Western markets. Consumers continue to differentiate between competitive offerings on the basis of more product information than has ever been available before. This drives companies further in the search for that value-added, perceived and valued by the customer. Peter Drucker, the well-known management author and visionary, has termed this search for value-added the new 'transnational ecology', an environment which does not recognize national boundaries any more than it does money or information (1989). Increasingly nations can be seen simply to be reacting to events in transnational money and capital markets rather than being able to shape them. Drucker sees traditional factors of production such as land and labour as being secondary to management. In this new environment the nation-state is but one of four units capable of effective economic policy for there is, too, an increasing shift of power to the region, as with the European Community. The third autonomous unit comprises the world economy of money, credit and investment flows organized by information that crosses national frontiers easily. Finally there is the transnational enterprise, not as large as we had once feared, which views the world as one market in which to produce and sell goods. The term that Drucker uses, 'transnational ecology', creates awareness and concern for our endangered habitat which require international policies so that we may protect our world from ourselves. Drucker sees interdependence as vital to our future.

Affluence does not bring literacy, thus product standardization

Table I.1   Levels of competitiveness.

Level	Example
1. Major trade zone	Japan and Southeast Asia, Western Europe, North America
2. Country	Ranking of Canada versus OECD countries, in broad economic measures (political stability or inflation)
3. Region	Location within several North American regions (Southern Ontario/Northeastern United States, or British Columbia/Western United States)
4. Industry	World market share, as measured by import/export ratios
5. Company	Value added by products
6. Department or activity	Benchmarking the relative cost per activity transaction or order
7 Employee skills	Education and literacy levels

Reprinted from an article appearing in *CMA Magazine* by Reuben Sokol, September 1992 issue, by permission of the Society of Management Accountants of Canada.

cannot be assumed. Prosperity is tied in with the fortunes of our buyers as well as our suppliers. Interdependence can never be ignored or forgotten.

Adapting to the global marketplace is increasingly a requirement: the global market is no longer an option. At the same time, it also has to be recognized that there is no particularly 'good' time that is better than any other in which to participate. Sokol (1992) put forward seven levels of competitiveness, ranging from the level of a major trade area to the detailed or functional level of a single employee (see Table I.1).

It has already been established that exporters will choose to export first to those markets which are psychologically close to their own domestic market, before venturing to those markets which, although geographically close, may be deemed to be more foreign. Michael Porter, the Harvard economist, has focused on the need for exporters to be successful first in their own domestic market (1990). Porter takes the view that they therefore export on the basis of a domestic advantage. Ohmae, who writes about the borderless economy (1985, 1990), focuses instead on the need to be an insider within the 'Triad' of the Western developed world: in other words, North America, Europe and Japan. In world trade there is no level playing field. Trade is still within the developed world for products developed for sophisticated affluent markets. Free trade is still only a concept to be implemented, whether we look at the European

Community or North America. In periods of economic expansion some degree of free trade may be countenanced, but it is still just an idea whose time is yet to come.

In the pages that follow, the skills required, the homework to be done and the constraints to be surmounted are discussed. International marketing is not a luxury to be considered as a bonus on top of domestic sales, but is a necessary part of the portfolio of every company seeking to sustain its own economic future. It therefore requires commitment and an equal share of the allocation of resources that would normally be committed to the domestic market. Certainly, it lacks definition and a body of knowledge sufficient to excite, but it is because companies do not recognize the importance and need for international marketing that there is this lack of suitable positions for those students of international marketing. Not all countries, however, hold international marketing in the same low esteem. While this may be true of the United Kingdom and of North America, it is not true of Japan where industry and commerce have maintained traditionally strong ties with its universities. Coincidentally, Japan has been forging ahead in international markets even in those countries in which it is not a traditional supplier. Need we look closer? The answer is undoubtedly yes. Only your fears are holding you back. Over the course of this book, let us try to dissipate and quantify those fears.

1

People

Too often in the past the only people recognized by management have been the supposed customers, to the sole exclusion of all other groups including the employees at the customer interface. This lack of an integrated vision of how to serve customer markets leads only to sub-optimization in terms of market representation. Failing to recognize or, to use the current term, 'empower' one's own employees at the 'sharp end' of the business – the customer interface – breeds confusion in the minds of customers, and disenchantment and hostility in the minds of employees.

Companies have come to recognize belatedly that the idea of just selling into a market and expecting success is hopelessly naive. First, there are few products that effectively sell themselves unless there is a massive shortage. Second, given all the incentives to subvert the channels of distribution set in place, a company with such a traditional mind-set could only be heading for potential customer alienation. Success and therefore loyalty, then, could be measured in terms of lack of a credible competitor. Customer loyalty cannot be taken for granted. Assume that loyalty is the absence of a better alternative and plan your strategy accordingly. 'Word of mouth' remains the most formidable of all promotional tools and yet it is the hardest for marketers to manipulate to their whim. There is generally too much 'noise', too many compelling competitive messages for other products from other producers, foreign and domestic, for one manufacturer's product to rise above them all unless it has some exceptional characteristic. People therefore make or break branded products with their perceptions of them and how they relate those perceptions to others.

Jasper Carrott, the Birmingham comedian, has for a long time enjoyed making fun of the Yugoslavian-made car, the 'Yugo', which is based on an outdated Fiat design. An example of his acid humour is: 'What do you call a Yugo convertible?' – 'A skip!' Such a perception set in the minds of customers everywhere will make them downgrade their estimation of this car and question whether it is the right car for them to be seen driving. Even by association, there may be strongly negative peer group pressure as to what to buy, what to drive, and this pressure which exists in all societies will filter down into brand preferences.

The other fact of life that is apparent to consumers and resellers, but not necessarily to producers, is that the service element in any product sale is becoming increasingly important. From product knowledge through to demonstration, installation and after-sales advice and service, this total service element is now, in many sectors of commerce, eclipsing the product itself. In the minds of consumers, service differentiates resellers who have otherwise identical products for sale. Service is a prime means of differentiating oneself in the market, but service depends on people. For them to function effectively they need to be empowered, to be delegated with the authority to deal with problems that arise at the customer interface. Being able to offer quality service is a prime determinant of long-term profitability, but it means that the company has to be fully integrated in its objective, that everyone accepts and is prepared to work towards the aim of excellence in service and that this is the message that will be communicated to the media through traditional advertising and also, one hopes, word of mouth. Service quality will depend upon the level of representation the company has in the foreign market, whether it is directly controlled or third-party. Level of representation and customer care policy should be incorporated into any agreement signed with a distributor or agent.

First and foremost, before any further discussion can take place, is the need for market research that identifies the wants and needs of the populace. There is an important distinction between 'wants' and 'needs', and the marketer who is able to exploit this successfully has a great deal to gain. In any purchase decision, one characteristic will generally be traded off against another. For example, consumers want a comfortable, reliable car which will accommodate the family, is inexpensive to run and maintain, and falls within their price range. More than one characteristic here may be traded against another. However, before examining individual consumer choices, we have to establish whether the market at large is viable. Basically, there are three elements to consider:

1. Market measurement determining the existing size and future potential of the market.
2. Comprehensive studies of all those presently in the market or about to enter the market.
3. Environmental studies, e.g. political, social, economic and legal.

We have to come up with some measures of market size and of its dynamism. Regarding a market for cars, we would need to ascertain not only how many new cars were registered in the last year, but how many were of domestic as opposed to imported origin, and the median price paid for a new car that year. Figures relating to consumer disposable income, family expenditure surveys and trends in spending patterns, as well as economic figures relating to the retail index and prevailing and forecast levels of inflation, plus product-specific legislation and constraints would all need to be known. Many of these points could be found in a library search, or increasingly, in a computer search of databases.

The secondary data search is essentially a trawl through published sources of information, including government as well as industry-related statistics.

1. Domestic consumption which is equal to domestic production less exports, but plus imports.
2. Personal disposable income, median consumer purchase prices and frequency of purchase.
3. Levels of demand, whether high/low and whether sustainable.
4. Available channels of distribution, rebate and discount structure within the trade. Strengths and weaknesses of the existing distribution channel.
5. Opportunities for alternative channels of distribution.
6. Buying patterns in terms of deciders, users and influencers. In the last ten years many producers have overlooked just how many young, single, professional women are driving their own cars. The car producers have not altered their promotional policies to really take advantage of the female car buyer and user. Similarly, how important is the trade press? How do people decide on price, on availability or on objective criteria, e.g. safety? Partly this will reflect cultural values as well as taxation levels (e.g. if the engine has a large cubic capacity) and legislation (e.g. safety such as mandatory rear seat belts, safety

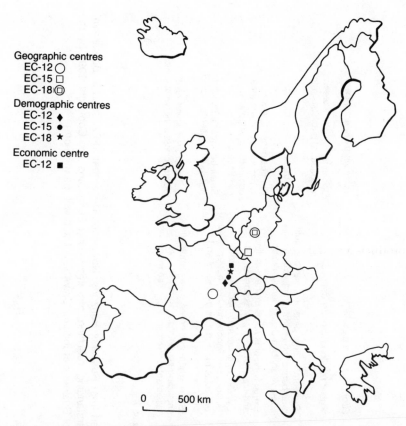

Geographic centres
EC-12 ○
EC-15 □
EC-18 ◎

Demographic centres
EC-12 ♦
EC-15 ●
EC-18 ★

Economic centre
EC-12 ■

0   500 km

Figure 1.1 Europe's new centres. (Reprinted from *Business Horizons*, January–February 1989, Sandra Vandermerwe and Marc André L'Huellier, 'Euro Consumers in 1992'. © Copyright 1989 by the Foundation for the School of Business at Indiana University. Used with permission.)

cage protecting the passenger shell from being crushed in a roll-over accident, daytime lights, etc.).

Also, do the specialist car magazines act as 'gatekeepers' in the sense of channelling objective information, or are they seen in a negative sense, screening out certain brands of manufacture? Is there a cultural sensitivity to any particular country of origin? Is 'foreignness' a disadvantage or can it be an advantage? Is it perceived as being linked with good design, styling, safety and reliability or with just the opposite?

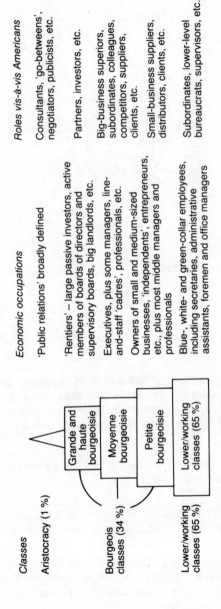

Classes

Aristocracy (1 %)

Bourgeois classes (34 %)
- Grande and haute bourgeoisie
- Moyenne bourgeoisie
- Petite bourgeoisie

Lower/working classes (65 %)
- Lower/working classes (65 %)

Economic occupations

'Public relations' broadly defined

'Rentiers' – large passive investors, active members of boards of directors and supervisory boards, big landlords, etc.

Executives, plus some managers, line- and-staff 'cadres', professionals, etc.

Owners of small and medium-sized businesses, 'independents', entrepreneurs, etc., plus most middle managers and professionals

Blue-, white- and green-collar employees, including secretaries, administrative assistants, foremen and office managers

Roles vis-à-vis Americans

Consultants, 'go-betweens', negotiators, publicists, etc.

Partners, investors, etc.

Big-business superiors, subordinates, colleagues, competitors, suppliers, clients, etc.

Small-business suppliers, distributors, clients, etc.

Subordinates, lower-level bureaucrats, supervisors, etc.

(Note: These percentages are rough estimates.)

Figure 1.2 Europe's social structure. (Reprinted from *Business Horizons*, November–December 1992, Jean J. Boddewyn, 1992, 'Fitting socially in Fortress Europe: Understanding, reaching, and impressing Europeans', © Copyright 1992 by the Foundation for the School of Business at Indiana University. Used with permission.)

	External information	Internal information
Operational decisions	Customer satisfaction measurement	Customer profitability analysis
Strategic decisions	Competition analysis. Segments on needs and values	Competence analysis

Figure 1.3 Monitoring the customer base. (Source: Mikael Paltschik and Kaj Storbacka, 1992, 'Monitoring the customer base to achieve profitability', *Marketing and Research Today*, **20** (3), p. 160.)

As we move down this market research list of desirable information, it becomes harder and harder to find relevant data from published sources of information. However, the basic viability of the market can be assessed first through published sources of information, before the necessary fieldwork is undertaken in the foreign market to gauge the answers to the questions above.

In any event, it is rare that secondary data will be directly comparable to data collected in one's own country. This is due to the fact that the prime source of statistics is government, collecting for its own benefit. Statistical bases are often just traditional. Cut-off points may relate to the age of schooling, which differs from country to country, or to the age of maturity which in some countries varies between 18 and 21 years of age. Again, depending upon the demographics, all people over 60 may simply be grouped together or there may be a few separate groups beyond that. It will depend to a certain degree on the size of that particular age group and its relative economic importance to the rest of that particular society.

Segmentation

As with segment identification anywhere, there are five criteria which identify whether or not you have a segment:

1. Size.

2. Measurability.
3. Accessibility.
4. Ability to buy.
5. Willingness to buy.

Without the presence of all five criteria, there is no viable segment. Segments can be identified demographically, psychographically (e.g. lifestyles, attitudes and beliefs – and here SRI's VALS segmentation profile of the nation is important) or geographically.

Another approach is benefit segmentation, where we seek to identify gaps in the existing market by importance of product attribute. Benefit segmentation has one clear advantage in that it is based upon predictive causal factors (rather than the descriptive factors above) which may form the basis for clustering. Haley undertook such a study of benefit segmentation in 1963, applying it to toothpaste. In segmentation, marketing's most powerful weapon, every single possible means of segmentation should be investigated. Syndicated sources such as SRI's VALS typology and Yankelovich, Skelly and White's monitor* are used to track consumer needs, but there are difficulties in trying to translate these typologies into product user groups. These typologies supplement and complement in-house research but do not supplant it.

Consumers	Marketers
Highest quality at lowest practicable price (value)	Highest-quality consumers at lowest incentive cost
Better control over their own *time*	Better control over marketing communications process
More personalized, customized product/service solutions	A rationalized system of resource allocation

Figure 1.4 An emerging confluence of needs? (Source: Robert A. Schmitz and Marc L. Rovner, 1992, 'A world of diminishing distance: How information technology is collapsing the transaction barriers between marketers and consumers', *Marketing and Research Today*, **20** (4), p. 234.)

*Yankelovich, Skelly and White, based in Madison Avenue, New York, conduct an annual survey nationwide across the USA each year known as the 'Yankelovich Social Monitor'. It monitors 40 specific social trends grouped into 10 key types.

Negotiation

A contract takes place when two parties reach agreement. Before that agreement can be reached, much time may be taken up with negotiations. Some cultural elements enter here in that it may be the expected cultural norm to haggle over price and to refuse to accept fixed list prices.

Increasingly, however, we are seeing a difference in the nature of the buyer–seller relationship. Internationally, what buyers expect of their suppliers is changing, due to changes in industrial practices such as single source of supply, just-in-time, and vendor quality rating programmes. New behavioural patterns are emerging now where the purchaser tries to persuade the supplier to provide and not vice versa. Theodore Levitt of the Harvard Business School wrote about this in a very influential article, 'After the sale is over', which appeared in the *Harvard Business Review* in the September–October issue of 1983. Using the analogy of a marriage, Levitt compared the perspectives of the buyer and the seller at each stage, from before the sale to long after the sale had been concluded. There was no convergence in the perspectives of either party; in fact, they diverged greatly at each successive stage.

Suppliers may be long-standing, established suppliers who have a relationship with a particular client that extends over many years. The expectations of buyer and seller on either side may be different, but if they are working together in a relationship that is close and harmonious, they will not be so materially different. What is new, however, is the expectation of the client that the suppliers invest their capital to develop a new component or sub-assembly for him

Table 1.1 How seller and buyer perspectives differ at each stage of a sale.

Stage of sale	Seller	Buyer
1. Before	Real hope	Vague need
2. Romance	Hot and heavy	Testing and hopeful
3. Sale	Fantasy-bed	Fantasy-board
4. After	Looks elsewhere for next sale	'You don't care'
5. Long after	Indifferent	'Can't this be made better?'
6. Next sale	'How about a new one?'	'Really?'

Reprinted by permission of *Harvard Business Review*. A table from Theodore Levitt (1983), 'After the sale is over', *Harvard Business Review*, September–October. Copyright © 1983 by the President and Fellows of Harvard College; all rights reserved.

Table 1.2 Purchaser profiles.

Criterion	Traditional purchaser	Reverse-marketing oriented
Action orientation	Responsive	Proactive
Outlook – way of thinking	Unidimensional thought	Multidimensional thought
Functional analysis	Routine approach	Creative approach
Perception of role within organization	Functionally limited view	Organizationally integrated view
Attitude towards supplier	Adversarial: 'them vs. us'	Cooperative partnership
Temporal horizon	Short-term perspective	Long-term perspective
Payoff horizon	Immediate and satisfying	Continuing and optimizing
Negotiation approach	Passive	Assertive
Motivation	Accepts status quo	Highly motivated

Reprinted by permission of the publisher from 'How reverse marketing changes buyer–seller roles', by David L. Blenkhorn and Peter M. Banting, *Industrial Marketing Management*, vol. 20, p. 189. © 1991 by Elsevier Science Publishing Co. Inc.

or her. This effectively transfers some of the role and cost of product development from the client to the supplier. Established suppliers with relationships that are long-standing and institutionalized will meet their clients' needs in terms of investment and adaptations which are non-contractual. This is what is meant by adaptive behaviour. It requires a different kind of outlook: not the passive-reactive approach, but a proactive orientation which looks at a payback period as ongoing within a close, harmonious relationship. This approach is so different from traditional marketing practice that the term 'reverse marketing' has been used, as the proposition comes not from the seller but from the client. Nevertheless, a few points have to be emphasized with regard to negotiations.

There are no agreed rules to negotiation, expectations are entirely subjective and situations are understood through perceptions. Yet a common mistake is to accept the very first offer made without attempting to beat the price down in any way. This means that you may be paying more than you would otherwise have done. Go into a negotiation round aware of your mandate and your time con-straints. If you are in a hurry to conclude an agreement, you will conclude a bad one. Gain leverage instead by holding something back for later negotiations, as revealing all or making early conces-sions may well be viewed as weakness. Again, communications can become difficult because of strategic misrepresentation and a low level of trust. Be proactive, not reactive. Do not be complacent or simply complain, but actively negotiate a possible solution instead.

Finally, everything that is verbally agreed must be set down in writing in specific detail. Negotiation is seen as conflict resolution and therefore invites the use of intimidation tactics and the use of time constraints in forcing a deadlock over negotiations. Negotiators are required to be steadfast, resolute and credible, whether bidding low as a buyer or selling high as a supplier, but never resorting to the use of the local language unless to exchange social pleasantries.

Sales

As sales are often viewed as the sole objective and the end to the means, it is becoming increasingly important to understand the customer: who he or she is; why, how and where they buy; the frequency with which they buy; and the use to which they put this product purchase. There is no easy short cut in learning about the needs and wants of the customer, but it is the only way in which sales can be assured. When working within one's own domestic market there is a good deal that can be assumed, but when you take a company product to another market you are effectively starting again, even if the end use is similar or even identical, for conditions of use will vary. Take the very simple example of cookbooks. These are bought all over the world and, by following the instructions, just about everyone can prepare a meal to the standards of Delia Smith – unless, of course, they live at a high altitude such as in Calgary, Canada, where extra cooking time has to be allowed to compensate for the altitude. The message is, simply, do not assume; find out about the market, and do not even begin to believe that, because the market in question is English-speaking, you share the same language. As Winston Churchill put it, Great Britain and the United States are two great nations divided by a common language!

In the target market the salesperson will be expected to perform basically the same duties as may be expected in the domestic market. There will be some degree of missionary selling required, some troubleshooting, some customer follow-up, perhaps even some delivery, and of course order-taking. Demand creation is therefore just one all-too-conspicuous part of the sales function. The nature of the task required has to be viewed alongside one's choice of resident company salesperson, commission agent or appointed dealer. Each option has its merits but, added to this, there are other factors to consider such as age, experience, personal network and motivation. Personal qualities are often most important in the resident foreign salesperson, who requires not only language, industrial contacts and good product knowledge, but also tenacity and a will to succeed, often in the face of impossible odds which he or she as a local national will at least be able to quantify. An excellent source here is Roger Axtell, who for twenty-three years was vice-president of Worldwide Marketing for the Parker Pen Company and spent most of that time abroad; he recounts the lessons that experience taught him in two popular books (1989; 1990).

Checklist: be aware

Arrogance

With company size comes arrogance; watch out for this.

Bribery

A label used often by the developed world to describe a common practice in many less developed countries of 'lubricating the administrative machinery'. Note that the equivalent word in the local language will usually fail to reflect the pejorative connotations of the word 'bribe' as perceived by one's shareholders or by politicians in one's own domestic market.

Communication

Essential at all levels. Used to be just newsletters, but with computerization and desktop publishing there is no reason why greatly improved communication cannot be provided. It is important to both recognize and reward achievement in some way and to acknowledge this throughout the company organization, thus minimizing 'psychic' or 'psychological' distance that occurs in all large organizations.

Consumers

They also differ in terms of what they buy, in what quantity, who makes the purchase decision, when and where they buy and how they pay for it. Consumer disposable income is only a partial explanation, as North America is kept afloat on 'plastic' money, not dollar bills!

Entrepreneurs

They are not universally liked. In developing countries they may be seen to be the 'black marketeers'. In developing economies a link with such a type could have effects exactly opposite to what you had intended because no one really trusts these 'wheeler-dealers'. Ensure that the entrepreneurs with whom you deal are honest and law-abiding as well as creative.

Ethnic groups

Ensure that no one will be offended or, worse, insulted by the product, its appearance, packaging, advertising or promotion.

Exhibitions

A very good way to meet people interested in your product and company, as well as to review competitors and their offerings.

Family

The concept of the family varies across cultures. In many, the concept of the 'extended family' may perhaps cover everyone sharing the same religion. In joint ventures this can lead to pressures to find work for many of these people.

Gifts

Have a different significance and importance depending on the culture of the country being visited. Generally, small gifts are acceptable, but large gifts may in some cases be seen as a 'bribe'.

Human performance

People do not always perform as they should, hence the need for a legal system which includes both civil and criminal law. See also 'Motivate and involve'.

Language

Local language can be a bonus for social use but if not fluent, do not attempt to discuss any part of a contract detail in anything other than your own language. Watch for legal constraints or product labelling and packaging which require the local language to be used and may forbid any other language to appear on the labelling.

Motivate and involve

Essential function, particularly wherever an intermediary is used. Company news and new product releases, supplies of brochures, catalogues, etc.

Ongoing training

This should be provided regularly at the home base to reward, familiarize and involve foreign staff in the field of developments.

Overseas visits

Need to be well planned. Goodwill is scarce and generally insufficient to sustain a company visit over a few days. Read correspondence, invoices and quarterly sales statements to familiarize yourself. Mutually agree a convenient date and try to ensure a two-way flow of communication – invite your buyer's or agent's criticisms and honest comments. On your side, propose suggestions for increasing business, e.g. potential customers, and visit clients with your distributor/agent.

Population statistics

Either a 'feast or famine' situation. Either totally unreliable, infrequently produced or else a plethora which will require some interpretation. Background reports such as the 'OBR' series (Overseas Business Reports produced by the US Department of Commerce) and those from the NTIS (another US organization) provide much useful data. Country-based banks also provide good economic background data but these tell you very little about product prospects.

Processing orders   Ensure that this is done with the minimum of delay. Install a contact person at head office to troubleshoot for foreign subsidiaries and their customers.

Sales meetings   Should be arranged to exchange information.

Social class   Use of lifestyle marketing encourages individuals to 'trade up'. Absolutely no one trades down unless perhaps in response to a plea on Third World poverty.

Xenophobic subjectivity   The more dissimilar the foreign market you own, the
of management   more likely it is that xenophobic instincts will arise.

References and further reading

Axtell, Roger E. (1989), *The Do's and Taboos of International Trade*, John Wiley: New York

Axtell, Roger E. (1990), *Do's and Taboos Around the World*, John Wiley: New York

Blenkhorn, David L. and Peter M. Banting (1991), 'How reverse marketing changes buyer–seller roles', *Industrial Marketing Management*, 20, p. 189

Boddewyn, Jean J. (1992), 'Fitting socially in Fortress Europe: Understanding, reaching, and impressing Europeans', *Business Horizons*, November–December, pp. 35–44

Drucker, Peter F. (1989), *The New Realities*, Butterworth-Heinemann: Oxford

Haley, Russell J. (1963), 'Benefit segmentation: A decision oriented research tool', *Journal of Marketing*, July, pp. 30–5

Harris, Philip R. and Robert T. Moran (1991), *Managing Cultural Differences*, 3rd edn, Gulf: Houston, TX

Hirschhorn, Larry and Thomas Gilmore (1992), 'The new boundaries of the boundaryless corporation', *Harvard Business Review*, May–June, pp. 104–15

Kennedy, Gavin (1984), *Everything is Negotiable!*, Hutchinson: London

Kosaka, Hiroshi (1992), 'A global marketing strategy responding to national cultures', *Marketing and Research Today*, 20 (4), pp. 245–56

Kotler, Philip (1986), 'Megamarketing', *Harvard Business Review*, 64 (2), pp. 117–25

Levitt, Theodore (1983a) 'After the sale is over', *Harvard Business Review*, September–October, pp. 87–93

Levitt, Theodore (1983b), *The Marketing Imagination*, Macmillan: New York

Norton, Rob (1993), 'Will tough talk mean trade wars?', *Fortune*, **127** (5), pp. 93–7

Ohmae, Kenichi (1990), *The Borderless World: Power and strategy in the interlinked economy*, HarperCollins: New York

Paliwoda, Stanley J. (1993), *International Marketing*, 2nd edn, Butterworth-Heinemann: Oxford

Paltschik, Mikael and Kaj Storbacka (1992), 'Monitoring the customer base to achieve profitability', *Marketing and Research Today*, **20** (3), pp. 155–67

Porter, Michael E. (1990), *The Competitive Advantage of Nations*, Macmillan: London

Schmitz, Robert A. and Marc L. Rovner (1992), 'A world of diminishing distance: How information technology is collapsing the transaction barriers between marketers and consumers', *Marketing and Research Today*, **20** (4), pp. 227–36

Vandermerwe, Sandra and Marc-André L'Huellier (1989), 'Euro-consumers in 1992', *Business Horizons*, January–February, p. 39

2

Process

Each company will undergo a different process. First, it is a question of whether a company is proactive in seeking new markets or reactive – simply going abroad because there is nowhere else to go. Success abroad depends upon planning, commitment and motivation. Apart from 'dumping', which is illegal in most Western countries (but difficult and slow to establish which is why it continues), most forms of market entry require an investment in resources and time.

Later I will discuss in turn the various modes of market entry, but for now it is worth considering some of the factors that are involved, and hence bear a cost, in servicing a foreign market.

1. Time zone differences relative to head office, which mean that certain key personnel will have to adjust their work hours to local foreign markets. This may mean working afternoons and evenings or else starting very early in the morning, some hours before the rest of the office.

2. Technology such as fax, telephone answering machines, voice mail and E-mail (electronic mail) can do much to minimize these time zone differences and reduce the psychological distance between the domestic market and the foreign target market.

3. Language, even when dealing with another English-speaking country, can create some complications. Technical jargon may be different from that used in the domestic market, and

colloquial expressions used at home may have a different or even no meaning in the foreign market in question. In Britain a product may 'go like a bomb' (i.e. be successful), but in the United States a product that 'bombed' is a disaster! Another example is where a committee may decide 'to table' a suggestion that has come up in discussion. This would mean adding it to the agenda in Britain, but in the United States it would mean shelving it! Quality translation is important.

4. Set-up costs vary from country to country due to costs of office space, and also perhaps due to restrictions relating to the employment of foreign nationals and the need to employ local nationals; difficulties of sourcing key ingredients or components when an import substitution policy is in place; inflation; economic and political uncertainty; the need for facilitating payments to bureaucrats; wage and price controls, and so on. The differences may make even the strong-hearted tremble.

5. Holiday allowance may be three weeks in North America, but is often five in Europe. France does not have a week in May without a holiday. Elsewhere in Europe, August may be seen as a 'write-off', as everyone is on holiday.

6. Company cars are seen as part of an executive remuneration package in Europe, but not elsewhere. From relatively junior to senior levels of management, the trend in Europe has been for companies to provide cars. This does not happen in North America.

7. Bureaucracy is everywhere, and varies only by degree. Certain less developed countries may seem to have more bureaucracy than others, whereas in fact it is just that they have a less committed workforce. Something, not necessarily work, expands to fill the working day, but that urgent application of yours may still be lying at the bottom of a pile that is not moving. What can you do to expedite matters? Facilitating payments may be common, but this may raise ethical questions as well as practical considerations relative to what may be seen to be a societal norm. There is no country in the world in which bribery and corruption are liked or condoned. It may well just be a matter of degree, but it is a concern for the international executive and his or her head office.

8. Expatriates usually accompany any initial establishment of a foreign subsidiary so as to ensure coordination and control. The costs of expatriates plus increasing levels of employment

legislation in the less developed countries (LDCs) have reduced their number. One 1993 estimate of the cost of sending an expatriate abroad was $250,000 because of built-in factors such as schooling, guaranteed trips home, car and pension plan (which, as in the case of France, may extend to 30 per cent of the salary).

9. Differences in quality standards and technical standards are bound to arise. Concentrating just on the negative aspects will produce a negative response. The key to success is to assess the degree to which local differences will change a standardized product and the costs that will be incurred. Working on similarities rather than on what divides us is a more feasible approach to international marketing.

10. Environmental issues relate to the degree of 'foreignness' of the company to that market, the degree of 'newness' of the product in question to the target market and the general political, economic and social agenda. Environmentalism is a connected issue. It involves not just the mandatory requirement to recycle but also, for the manufacturer who is responsible for this packaging, the legal responsibility also for its disposal.

11. Freight. The question is not simply the cost of our freight versus sea freight or multi-modal. There are distinct cost-saving benefits attached to air freight which compensate to some degree for the higher price. Export packing is less, the duration of time in transit is significantly reduced and air freight can even constitute a competitive advantage, offering the foreign customer the security of an unrivalled level of customer service. Moreover, just-in-time delivery of this kind eliminates the need for expensive warehousing and goods-handling inventories are kept low as well.

These factors are but some of those that come into play in international marketing and – let us be clear here – international marketing as opposed to just simply opportunistic exporting implies presence and a commitment to the foreign target market. Terms tend to lose their significance quickly when not sufficiently well defined at the outset.

The term 'marketing' has become devoid of meaning. Those elements that incorporate a consumer orientation have been absorbed into the 'quality revolution' and the move towards TCS

Table 2.1 Thirteen prominent trends that will shape marketing to 2000 AD: results of a worldwide Delphi study.

Cluster 1	Environment	(2.64)
	Globalization	(2.53)
	Trading blocs/regionalism	(2.44)
Cluster 2	Technology	(2.38)
	Services	(2.30)
	Human	(2.29)
	Central Europe	(2.27)
	Pacific Rim	(2.26)
Cluster 3	Third World	(2.20)
	World finance	(2.02)
	Foreign direct investment	(1.90)
	International trade framework	(1.90)
	Energy	(1.72)

Note: This was a Delphi study of twenty-nine exports in business, government and academia in the United States, Japan and Western and Central Europe. They ranked their choice of key issues on a three-point scale for 'high', 'medium', or 'low' importance and impact.

Source: Michael R. Czinkota and Ilkka A. Ronkainen (1992), 'Global marketing 2000: A marketing survival guide', *Marketing Management*, **1** (1), Winter, pp. 36–45.

(total customer satisfaction). A strategic marketing focus should incorporate both a quality orientation and an internal marketing focus so as to motivate, involve and empower the entire workforce.

The commonly described process of either moving one's goods into a foreign market or distributing within a foreign market even to point-of-sale is not one that is convincing in terms of customer orientation. There is usually a belief or 'hunch' that this is a good product or a good price and so people will buy. Sound facts, even common sense, are missing. Hard-nosed business people, once they become committed to a project, will switch off their common sense and fail to realize the time costs of their pet projects. For example, in any costing it would be quite acceptable practice to include some figure for management time. This is seldom done, so in fact the pet project then escapes some of the costs which must then be borne by other product lines if the company is to stay afloat financially.

On the other hand, strict rules regarding a certain level of profitability within a given time frame impose unrealistic constraints on entry to a foreign market and bring economic ruin sooner rather than later. Do not fail to take account of all costs incurred, even if you do not consider them to be costs. There is always an 'opportunity' cost in that, if you are devoting your energies to one activity, you are possibly missing out on another. Likewise, remember that foreign markets are more difficult than the domestic market you have been dealing in and there is a lot to learn in terms of the business culture and the pace and nature of transactions demanded. Language, cultural norms, currency exchange and local legislation introduce complexity; these can be mastered but only over time, unless a foreign national is delegated to take control. This requires a willingness on the part of the domestic company both to devolve power and perhaps to accept different methods of operation from those used until now. Company orientation and willingness to devolve power or empower managers in the field are vital for international success.

Large multinationals benefit because of corporate services departments back at head office which can easily transfer resources and skills across countries. For small companies, there is no international resource base to which they can turn, and so the decision on whether to go or not becomes more complex. However, in terms of representation in the foreign market a small company can easily rival a large multinational in terms of size of representation. There is no world pattern common to multinationals or to small companies when it comes to foreign market entry. There is no single strategy that comes out on top in all situations, and so the advice is based upon the degree of fit that a given mode of market entry has with prevailing market conditions. This means taking a contingency approach, but also recognizing that nothing is held constant and that market entry, once decided, must be monitored and subjected to periodic checks for effectiveness and inevitable market change at some indeterminate point. It is not an evolution which would indicate an upwards movement in terms of size or resource allocation, but an evaluation which can decide appropriate resource investment levels either in terms of increasing, decreasing or withdrawing them completely.

The choice for foreign market entry is wide:

1. Indirect exporting via a buying house in your own domestic market.

2. Direct exporting via agent or distributor.

3. Mergers and acquisitions which give instant access to a foreign market.

4. Internal venturing – management buyout.

5. Joint venture, which used to be equity based but is now more

likely to be a strategic alliance as a research and development partnership.

6. Minority investment, which may be a defensive investment to secure a toehold in a potentially important foreign market.
7. Strategic alliances and cooperative agreements, not only for distribution but for research and production as well.
8. Research and development partnerships.
9. Cross-licensing and cross-distribution.
10. Franchising internationally a successful business idea already proven in the domestic market.
11. Formation of a consortium to engage in joint bidding activities, as in the offshore oil industry or construction industry.

Levels of competitiveness

Being a good domestic competitor today is insufficient. Any industry that exhibits both growth and some degree of value-added will have competition. Those competitors are not necessarily domestic either. Trade is the only economic activity that is expanding. With years of successive gains in growth, the effect has been to change permanently the very nature of competition. There is no industry without an international dimension. In basic economic texts, commodities are poorly regarded – yet look around at how water is marketed today across all markets. Sparkling or still waters then had flavours added, but the real value-added was introduced by Evian with a spray dispenser of natural water, which created a brand out of a commodity and raised its value to the equivalent in price of $5 an ounce. The differential advantage has often to be created. The problem with commodities is that there is very little room in which to manoeuvre. Oil may be termed 'light' or 'heavy crude', and this has implications also on price, but very often it is also identified by the source from which it came, e.g. North Sea Brent (light) or West Texas (intermediate). Commodities then become classified, but within that classification there is little room to manoeuvre the price: within that classification all suppliers are roughly equal. There is no opportunity for superior customer satisfaction. Marc Particelli of Booz, Allan and Hamilton has taken this further (1990), assessing competitive advantage through three dimensions: product, business

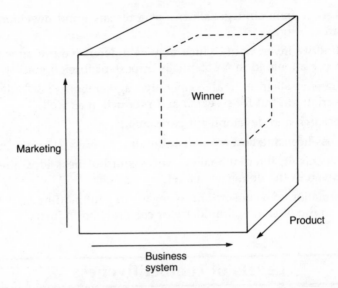

Figure 2.1   Framework: competitive advantage in three dimensions. (Source: Marc C. Particelli, 'A global arena', *Journal of Consumer Marketing*, **7** (4), Fall, p. 46.)

systems and marketing. The product is seen as the foundation of the business, but the business system is the means by which this product is conveyed to the final consumer as a package of benefits; and this is where marketing is important, in knowing what the customer wants and is seeking from the product. Particelli argues that only by achieving advantage across all three dimensions can a company achieve lasting market success but, in the global arena, instances where all three of these dimensions can be transferred without modification will rarely be found.

Export sales

First, there are a number of ways in which export sales can be achieved without any foreign presence or foreign agency or distributor network. Direct sale to end user and supply via mail order are but two of these ways. Equally, buying offices abroad may buy on behalf of their parent organizations – retailers, department stores or purchasing consortia in Australia, Europe, North America or the

Pacific Basin. Sales concluded in this way are, in effect, domestic sales to the producer. Only the product is going abroad and, in this case, without the active involvement of the manufacturer.

Sales of this kind often lead to a realization that the market abroad may indeed be larger than one's own present share of one's national market. This may give rise to market research in order to further ascertain the market potential and to take any necessary steps to protect the company's growth in that target market. Without this, continued export may be like pushing goods and services into a vacuum. There has to be market response, without which the company does not have a market – only a foreign inventory location. A purely reactive strategy makes you vulnerable to speed of market change and unable to capitalize on opportunity, because of lack of market information and weak, unresponsive market representation.

Exporting with local technical presence

Salespeople are often a law unto themselves. That which sets them apart is also, too often, their greatest weakness. They share an optimism and a confidence in themselves, greatly enhanced by their natural eloquence. Given the diversity of the tasks facing the salesforce, their skills are often sorely tried. They are expected to be missionary salespeople, troubleshooters, order-takers and, on occasion, delivery people as well. Their greatest weakness is often that they buy time, or just buy off customers with promises which they know are impossible to fulfil. When this extends into operating and technical specifications then the salespeople can often find themselves out of their depth. Technical requests should be met with factual replies, not glib answers, if there is to be any prospect of building relationships with these customers. Technical presence may be more costly, but can be justified where the following conditions prevail:

1. The company is in a 'problem child' category, i.e. everyone else in the market is doing much better than they are.
2. The company is foreign and its product, sales and service provision are unknown in the target market.
3. The product in question crosses many industrial applications and has also spawned a myriad possible new uses in recent years, many of which are still to be properly evaluated.

4. Where machinability is a factor, consumables may be bought in sufficient volume to last perhaps six months. This is a significant investment and outlay, and perceived risk has first to be greatly reduced to allow the sale to proceed.

5. Where salespeople already carry a large product range and have only rudimentary knowledge of each one.

6. Where all other things are equal in terms of product, service and price. The provision of a technical presence may provide not only reassurance, but a differential advantage. It is a form of commitment to the customer.

7. Socialization with technical personnel creates a further bond with the client's organization and may help to develop a client relationship.

Internationalization beyond exporting

Knowledge has become a global commodity, but it is not homogeneous. As Badaracco has pointed out (1991), it can either be 'migratory' or 'embedded'. If migratory, a design or a product concept, for example, can easily be transferred. Formulas, designs, books, manuals, even people who may retain this much-sought-after knowledge in question, can be transferred easily. Migratory knowledge can move extremely quickly. Embedded technology which resides, for example, in relationships or within company organizations, can move only slowly. Perhaps one individual has a greater understanding of the knowledge in question than all the others. This gives rise to a number of opportunities for leverage with the aim of securing the highest possible premium for the transfer of this particular knowledge.

With migratory knowledge just about anyone, with varying degrees of success, can set up a fast-food outlet. Technically it is possible. In practice, different standards will emerge. People will then turn to one company or one individual as the embodiment of that knowledge to help them learn and acquire what they need to know. In production it has been the case for many years that 'know-how agreements' have typically gone hand-in-hand with licensing deals, thereby transferring to another not only the right to produce using company-specific know-how which has been protected and patented, but also to incorporate the licensor's production experience and updates in actual production. Experience therefore becomes a tradable commodity. Migratory knowledge creates opportunities for others to copy, but the inability to copy or to acquire embedded knowledge other than through direct means has the result that success often eludes those who simply seek to copy product design wholesale. First, production experience in the innovative firm may have moved on quite significantly, posing a barrier to entry to the market to all would-be competitors. Second, the innovative company that created the design may have decided to change specifications quite dramatically once the design actually entered production. The early innovator was most probably in touch with the market at the time of product launch. Now we face the danger of the time lags that have taken place since the first product was launched, and the change in the buying public's attitudes since. When a product is first launched, innovation itself has an appeal, but after a very short time the buying public starts to become critical. A poor competitor then enters at this second stage with a commodity product that was really designed for stage one.

Knowing the market for which you are producing is vital and there are no easy short cuts to this. However, where speed is important, franchising and management contracts can offer the security of tried and tested systems. Admittedly these may now be under consideration for a new foreign market, but certain franchises have withstood this test of time in that their uniqueness has not dissipated. Franchises such as The Body Shop continue to enjoy success, while others such as Tie Rack are more vulnerable to market pressures as what they have to offer is less distinctive and therefore more vulnerable to competitive pressure.

Franchising is a good example of being able to market a tried and tested product or service. The importance of brand names rests in the reassurance that it brings to the consumer who not only recognizes it, but awards it with a premium. Brands extend beyond products to services such as hotels and the car rental business, where matching levels of service to the domestic market are expected. Conformance to a perceived level of service lies behind the success of the service or product brand. Franchising extends this internationally, allowing a successful domestic firm to penetrate foreign markets with shared capital while, for the franchisee, it opens up the possibility of entering into business, often for the first time, but using someone else's established brand name and operating procedures. The management contracts and support systems that accompany franchising are in large part responsible for the success of franchising internationally.

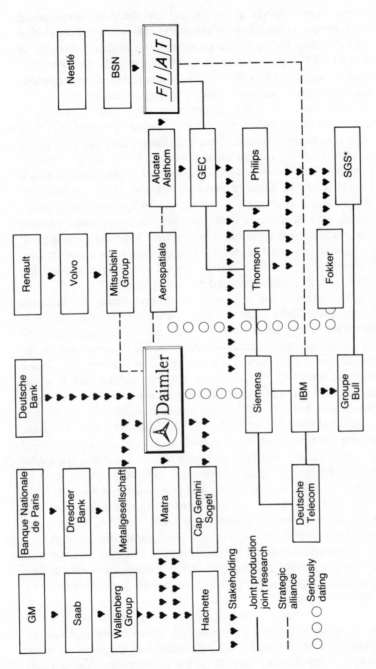

Note: *'SGS' major shareholder, Italy's Finmecannica, recently took a stake in Fokker.

Figure 2.2 European strategic alliances. Germany's Daimler-Benz and Italy's Fiat are at the centre of a web of cooperative deals being created by Europe's leading industrial companies in advance of the 1992 deadline for the single market. It's easier than competition. (Source: Peter Fuhrman, 1992, 'Getting in bed together', *Forbes*, 11 May, pp. 86–7.)

Elsewhere, embedded forms of knowledge can be seen to lead firms, often even arch-rivals within the same industry, to form strategic business alliances. Whereas a joint venture may be formed on a vertical relationship within a distribution channel, strategic alliances are often horizontal and involve research and development partnerships between companies that are near-equals.

Investment issues

The old style of thinking was to believe that factors of production were all important and that in the search for lower factor costs a company would travel the world, often moving global production to the lowest factor cost location. This also gave rise to the term 'runaway multinational' and perhaps creates to some degree the ambivalence with which multinational, or more commonly 'trans-national' or 'global', corporations are received today. In today's world market, production cost is often but a small percentage of the final selling price, insufficient to even consider alternative produc-tion locations. New economic arguments therefore have to be found to explain the paradox whereby societies least able to afford the manufactures they produce should become so specialized in their production.

Peter Drucker is perhaps the only current management thinker to have not only witnessed but commented on this important trend. Land, labour and materials are now secondary. Money is trans-national and national governments are reactive to monetary pres-sure, being directed by it rather than directing it. Drucker describes four partially dependent variables, linked and interdependent, but not controlled by each other. These include: the nation-states; the region, as in the European Community or NAFTA; an almost autonomous world economy of money, credit and investment flows; and the transnational enterprise which views the world as one market in which to both produce and sell goods and services. In this new scenario in which we now find ourselves, trade is becoming a function of investment and information has become a global commodity. This requires not only a knowledge of the market but also a base within it. These pressures apply to businesses of all sizes, but create an advantage for small to medium-sized enterprises which are able to move more freely, almost invisibly, across national boundaries relative to the highly conspicuous transnational corporations. This, then, can lead us to expect not only that the global economy will continue to manifest the same traits as today, but that certain of these will predominate. The economic rationale for certain actions changes, and so in the new global marketplace we can see an enhanced picture of what exists today with important international strategic alliances between small and medium-sized national domestic companies removing the need for both the transnational organization and for ownership as a proxy for control.

Checklist: be aware

Assess agents and distributors before signing a contract	Use chambers of commerce, departments of trade and banks, first to get lists of possible intermediaries you might use; then ask for some quantitative assessment of these organizations. Use foreign embassies and consulates and your own embassies and consulates overseas.
Awareness	Be aware of the implications of differences in the local market. You may have to change your work schedule so that you are available to take calls because of time differences, for example.
Complaints analysis	Can give rise to good market opportunities. Analyze complaints from a strategic focus. If you do not receive complaints, there is something wrong. Implement focus groups immediately.
Cultural sensitivity	Technology is not culturally sensitive, but language is. Watch for quality translation and xenophobia (as interpreted by the local market) in head office communications.
Franchising	Offers the franchisor an opportunity to expand internationally with a successful tried and tested market concept. Franchising extends to the franchisee the use of the brand name, the logo and all that is normally recognizable and associated with the franchisor in terms of design, packaging and presentation. Mistakes can be costly.
Ingrown industries	Mature industries where there is concentration in terms of suppliers are particularly prone to attack by predators coming from outside the industry. Incestuous cosy relationships are to be avoided – they are probably illegal anyway!

Introspection	Looking in the mirror instead of out of the window is a major cause of failures.
Legal	Review carefully with a lawyer in the foreign target market any sales contract, agency or distributorship agreement. Check also for product liability and exposure to other possible legal constraints including labelling, language and hiring practices.
Motivation	If new to a market, you, together with your agent, distributor, licensee or other partner, will require motivation, not just to succeed but to continue. This will depend to some degree on the goals which you initially set for yourself.
Resources	Assess the company's own resources realistically as to what your foreign markets will require each year for the next five years.
Respond to change	Change creates opportunities. Respond to it – do not be carried along by it.
Sale of excess production	Over-production is not a good rationale for looking internationally, but under-utilization of expensive resources is!
Saleable knowledge	Company-specific knowledge which is embedded within the company is a more saleable asset than industry-wide knowledge.
Speed now, pay later	Certain modes of foreign market entry such as the use of a commission agent offer almost instant access to a foreign market. However, it may be difficult to terminate an agent. Check the market beforehand as to long-term potential. If you want an agent, check all potential agents carefully.
Strategic alliances	Now found commonly throughout Europe in both vertical and horizontal forms of alliance.

References and further reading

Alexander, Nicholas (1990), 'Retailers and international markets: Motives or expansion?', *International Marketing Review*, 7 (4), pp. 75–85

Badaracco, Joseph L. (1991), *The Knowledge Link: How firms compete through strategic alliances*, Harvard Business School Press: Boston, MA

Czinkota, Michael R. and Ilkka A. Ronkainen (1992), 'Global marketing 2000: A marketing survival guide', *Marketing Management*, 1 (1), pp. 36–45

Drucker, Peter F. (1989), *The New Realities*, Butterworth-Heinemann: Oxford

Forsgren, Mats, Ulf Holm and Jan Johanson (1990), 'Internationalisation of the second degree', paper presented to the Academy of International Business UK Regional Conference, University of Strathclyde, Glasgow, 6–7 April

Fuhrman, Peter (1992), 'Getting in bed together', Forbes, 11 May, pp. 86–7

Johanson, Jan and Jan-Erik Vahlne (1990), 'The mechanism of internationalisation', International Marketing Review, 7 (4), pp. 11–24

Lee, Chong S. and Yoo S. Yang (1990), 'Impact of export market expansion strategy on export performance', International Marketing Review, 7 (4), pp. 41–51

Main, Jeremy (1989), 'How to go global – and why', Fortune, 28 August, pp. 70–6

Morita, Akio (1992), 'Partnering for competitiveness: The role of Japanese business', Harvard Business Review, May–June, pp. 76–83

Nelson, Carl A. (1990), Import/Export: How to get started in international trade, Liberty Hall Press: Blue Ridge Summit, PA

Particelli, Marc C. (1990), 'A global arena', Journal of Consumer Marketing, 7 (4), Fall, pp. 43–52

Sherlock, Paul (1992), 'The irrationality of "rational" business buying decisions', Marketing Management, 1 (2), Spring, pp. 9–15

Specks, Christine and Sundeep Sahay (1991), 'Segmentation of international markets for the remote sensing industry', Dimensions of International Business, 5, School of Business, Carleton University International Business Study Group, Ottawa, Spring, pp. 55–67

Valentine, Charles F. (1990), The Arthur Young International Business Guide, John Wiley: New York

Welch, Lawrence S. (1992), 'Developments in international franchising', Journal of Global Marketing, 6 (1/2), pp. 81–97

Wells, L. Fargo and Kevin B. Dulat (1990), Exporting from Start to Finance, Liberty Hall Press: Blue Ridge Summit, PA

Witcher, Barry J. (1990), 'A new kind of marketing for Europe', Durham University Business School, Occasional Paper Series no. 9064

Young, Stephen (1990), 'Internationalisation: Introduction and overview', International Marketing Review, 7 (4), pp. 1–8

3

Power

Corporate power: is it transferable?

Market power is not automatically transferable to other markets, and certainly not by right. Even amongst the many global and international companies, there are few truly global brands. Product needs may be similar across countries but in the delivery of the final and total product offering, costly mistakes are often made through a corporate arrogance that what succeeds at home will succeed elsewhere. For example, many American companies in consumer products are successful in Europe, but there are also many that have repeatedly failed to transfer their American home advantage into a profitable market niche in other markets. There may be many reasons for this, including variables that have not received sufficient weighting in the preliminary market investigations such as the following:

- Language, xenophobia and nationalistic influences.
- Personal disposable income which was never even approximately the same as per capita GNP. One (personal disposable income) is the measure of what the individual has to spend; the other (GNP) is the measure of national wealth per capita to which the individual may be restricted. Even purchasing power parties (PPP), while in many ways a good measure of assessing market potential, introduces a bias in terms of different factor costs.

- Product size and cost; so-called divisibility of the product making it affordable to the average consumer, but perhaps requiring modification in terms of size or price per unit.

- Store location, style of merchandising and level of service traditionally offered to customers, whether high or low.

- Information which is necessary for products bought infrequently, whether high or low value-added.

- Lack of socialization and familiarization with the use of sophisticated automated machinery as with automated teller machines (ATMs) outside banks, for example.

- Lack of credit, acceptance of 'plastic money' (credit cards) and different cultural norms related to credit and finance.

- Consumer demographics, buying patterns and lifestyle trends which may vary from one country to another.

Market power can be transferable, but it cannot be transposed wholesale. Companies such as Coca-Cola and Pepsi-Cola have only recently been able to penetrate the British market with their vending machines. The reason for this apparent lag behind the US market is simply that the British have not traditionally turned to canned drinks at break-time, preferring instead to drink mainly tea. It has taken time for the generation weaned on Coke and Pepsi – 'the baby boomers' – to come to the fore. One has to take account of the market being entered and there often has to be a translation of the market offering to suit the market in question, with few exceptions.

Market segmentation lends itself to effective internationalization. The identification of similar market segments will obviate the need for expensive product modification where market segments are virtually identical across markets. Lifestyles are a key issue here. There are many similarities that may be drawn in a comparison of capital-city dwellers in, for example, Spain, France and Britain. Urban populations may have segments that may be found in all cities. Segmentation studies that profile consumer-buying behaviour may well track similarities that exist across a number of markets, while to all outward appearances these markets remain very different, whether through political ideology, religion or traditional culture or some combination of all of these. To give an example, Whirlpool launched a pan-European advertising campaign in 1990 based on their clothes driers and dishwashers. Whirlpool have identified segments in Europe that span national frontiers, with labels for European homemaker types such as 'traditionalists' and

---

Common mistakes

- Do not underestimate the complexity of the market.
- Do not try to grow too fast.
- Do not fail to exercise the same business judgement that you would at home.
- Do not assume that having European nationals working for your operation will solve all of your cultural problems.
- Pay attention to the small print on letters of credit.
- Do not underestimate your product.

Source: Donna Brown (1990), 'Game-winning strategies for Europe's new market', *Management Review*, May, pp. 10–15. Reprinted by permission of publisher, from *Management Review*, May 1990. © 1990 American Management Association, New York. All rights reserved.

'aspirers'. Good ideas that have popular appeal and fulfil basic needs can enjoy rapid market success, but market power today rests more with the retailer than with the manufacturer. A telling example is that of Totes Inc., which came up with a new product idea by adding rubbery treads to heavy socks so as to provide traction and naming them 'slipper socks'. Within a year of product launch, Totes had total sales of 14 million pairs, of which K-Mart and Wal-Mart Stores Inc. accounted for 1.5 million pairs. However, within two years, those two retailers found suppliers who could make 'knock-off' (i.e. a close copy) slipper socks for less. They then dropped Totes Inc. as a supplier and lowered the price of their new version of the product by 25 per cent or more. The buying public remains loyal to these two discount retailers and the manufacturers cannot afford to ignore them because of the volume they handle. Meanwhile, the relative size of both the retailer base and the manufacturing base within the US economy is shrinking, but the essential consumer information coming through the electronic tills includes information on buying patterns which remains in the hands of the retailers. While the manufacturers continue to devote resources to the building of their brands, these discount stores focus on competitive pricing of a limited selection of products based on their customers' buying patterns and backed by computerized inventory management via the electronic check-outs. This system has been applied so successfully to different product categories that these discount stores have been termed 'category killers', and described as an unstoppable market force that could turn its market power to virtually any product category. Similar market power is to be found in retail sections in all other developed countries. In Europe, readjusting to the concept of the Single European Market, new alliances have been formed amongst national retailers in different retail sectors which will create new power balances with manufacturers that will have far-reaching and permanent effects. At the same time, the technology behind these retailers is continually improving, increasing data communication speeds from the current 9,600 bits per second to 64 kilobits per second through new telephone technology called ISDN (Integrated Services Digital Network). This means a strengthening of their computerized network of branches, extending into areas presently ignored. More information is being collected than before and we now need the computer power to disseminate this information quickly over the widest possible area so as to include even the farthest-flung sales branch. Meanwhile, within the US population there is a 'downshifting', as Grey Advertising termed it, by consumers. This is a structural change in shopping habits by consumers with less money to spend on purchases and with better product information than before who are able to perceive commodities of brands and so move instead to private labels and even generics. Many of these people are also now moving into the discount stores for the first time and like what they see, being able to purchase many well-established brands at discounted prices. This same trend can be seen in Western Europe.

While technology gives rise to many new products, it is not the only source of product innovation, nor does it account on its own for any of the subsequent product success. What is important is tapping into social trends and discovering the values that consumers attach to people, personalities and concepts. *Business Week* produces such a listing with regard to the United States each year (see Figure 3.1).

Fortune Products of the Year 1992

- The Nicotine Patch
- Hip-Hop Fashion
- Goodyear Aquatred Tire
- Ross Perot
- Chrysler LH Series
- AT & T Videophone
- Chocolate Chip Cookie Dough Ice Cream
- Sony Minidisc and Philips Electronics DCC (Digital Compact Cassette)
- Apple Computer Powerbook
- Eastman Kodak Photo CD

Source: Alison L. Sprout (1992), 'Products of the years', *Fortune*, 28 December, pp. 64–9. © 1992 Time Inc. All rights reserved.

WHAT'S IN   **WHAT'S OUT**

POLITICS & ECONOMICS

Investment	Consumption
Vision	The vision thing
First Lady lawyers	First Lady grandmas
Lloyd Bentsen	James Baker
Michael Kinsley	George Will
Latin America	Europe
Rhodes scholars	British Royals
Managed care	Extra lab tests
Teledemocracy	Photo ops
Socks	Millie

BUSINESS

Optimism	Gloom
George Steinbrenner	Marge Schott
Reengineering	Quality circles
Virtual corporations	Vertical integration
Core competencies	Diversification
Bloomberg Business News	Reuters
Muni-bond funds	Global-income funds
40 1(k) plans	ESOPs
Series EE savings bonds	CDs
Managed trade	Free trade
Silicon Valley	The Pentagon
Wrist braces	Carpal tunnel syndrome
15-year mortgages	30-year mortgages
Separate CEOs, chairmen	Cronyism

SOCIAL TRENDS

Jeffersonian populism	Hamiltonian elitism
Jerry Seinfeld	Woody Allen
Barney the Dinosaur	Big Bird
Denzel Washington	Bruce Willis
MTV's Tabitha Soren	*Meet the Press*
Dracula	Batman
Corelle	Fiestaware
Caffe Latte	Cappuccino
Goatees	Sideburns
Nickelodeon	Fox
Garage sales	Consumerism

Figure 3.1 US fashions in values. (Source: 'That's upbeat not beat-up', *Business Week*, 21 December 1992, p. 40. Reprinted from December 21, 1992 issue of *Business Week* by special permission, copyright © 1992 by Business Week Inc.)

Market power: can it be measured?

In terms of market share, yes, it can, but this is in terms of one market whereas we should be considering relative market share on an international or even global basis. Within one's own domestic market a company already has a certain limited knowledge of the market by virtue of the fact that it is based there. Almost as if by osmosis, a certain amount of market information will filter through, but this is not enough. Within the domestic market a company can conduct its own market research, by interviewing customers face to face as they enter sales outlets, mailing them questionnaires, telephoning them at work or by asking a market research agency to do the same or perhaps something a little different, branching out into focus groups that may well reveal highly useful data regarding the company's image and product market profile.

At home there may be consumer panels to tap into and various computer geodemographic systems available such as ACORN or Compusearch, which basically take a national market and segment it into different clusters using neighbourhood and socioeconomic profiles. Using these thirty-eight or forty-four key clusters, depending on which system you use, you can target customers with an ease that was not possible before. Computerization of these databases has led to an increase in direct mail marketing and to an irreversible decline in traditional print media campaigns. Going abroad, much of this information is simply not available. Yet, with computerization, anyone who has a computer and a modem and subscribes to Compuserve could access, through telephone numbers available across the world, any one of more than 850 databases.

Most of the information provided in the traditional international marketing literature is limited, hopelessly out of date and therefore dangerous. Not that open information is always a good thing, for marketers know that opportunities exist where markets are in disarray and no one is in supreme control. This can have a strong effect on demand patterns, prices charged and customer-supplier interaction.

As General Sir David Ramsbotham put it:

Intelligence and information gathering must be a continuous requirement and process in every walk of life, involving directed observation of one's potential opponent by using every surveillance and analysis means at one's disposal. Information is a force multiplier, and a resource that must be managed as a resource. (1993)

Ramsbotham has argued the similarities between the military and civilian management. He separates information into two types: strategic and tactical. Strategic information is gleaned from such sources as satellites, communications monitoring, aerial surveillance, the media and analysis of known opposition intentions and methods; tactical intelligence is gleaned by much lower-level sources likely to be under the control of the commander of a particular part of the battlefield. It is the commander's task to filter that which is useful and relevant from that which is somewhat extraneous to the situation.

Risk can also be minimized where similarities with one's own domestic market can be seen. There is more to be gained from a strategy of standardized segmentation across international markets than from anything else. Segmentation is the most significant weapon in the marketing armoury. It provides the opportunity for the well-prepared attack on a target market and also wards off competitors. Appealing to consumers across nations that share the same profile in terms of income, status and lifestyle is much safer than going into a foreign market with a shotgun approach, hoping to reach persons unknown, which is all that is achieved with an unfocused sales approach. International segmentation can be very effective and also reinforcing, in that the same product, perhaps with very similar if not identical packaging and communications, is seen to be available in foreign markets. This creates prestige and status and has a 'spill-over' effect into other markets as well, carried by consumers, not by the advertiser.

Market power of trading blocs

There is an interesting myth that nations trade but, in doing their best to promote national industry at the expense of international competitors, they create barriers to trade instead, seeking to make trade, particularly imports, disadvantageous. While tariff barriers have decreased over the years with the establishment of GATT in 1948, in many cases these have been replaced by non-tariff barriers

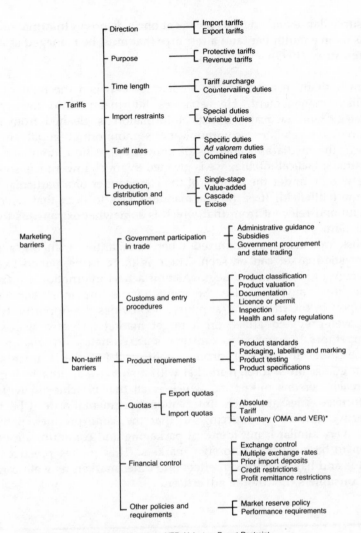

Note: *OMA: Orderly Marketing Agreement; VER: Voluntary Export Restraint.

Figure 3.2 Marketing barriers. (Source: Sak Onkvisit and John J. Shaw, 1988, 'Marketing barriers in international trade', *Business Horizons*, May–June, pp. 64–72. Reprinted from *Business Horizons*, May–June 1988. © Copyright 1988 by the Foundation for the School of Business at Indiana University. Used with permission.)

which have grown to such a proportion in times of recession as to threaten the very existence of GATT itself, now paralysed by inaction and an inability to deal effectively with trading disputes focused on non-tariff barriers that it was never mandated to deal with. Non-tariff barriers are much less visible but every bit as crippling in their effect as tariff barriers. Non-tariff barriers may be grouped as customs and entry procedures and involve classification, validation, documentation, licences, inspection and health and safety regulations. Products entering the country also have to meet that country's standards with regard to product standards, packaging, labelling, marketing, testing and specifications. To reduce, if not eliminate, these pressures, there has therefore been a move to standardize, coordinate and unify not only product standards, but trade procedures generally.

The European Community (EC) is the largest single trading bloc in the world today. The EC is a customs union moving closer towards harmonization and coordination of national member policies The EC now has signing authority on trade agreements for its member states. EFTA (European Free Trade Association) is a small grouping of countries like Switzerland which are anxious to maintain their neutrality. The position of EFTA towards the European Community is ambiguous. Not so long ago there were proposals to merge EFTA with the EC, but the people in Switzerland voted against that. Whether it formally goes ahead or not does not really matter, for a few members of EFTA have independently pushed for membership of the EC in their own right. There is therefore a large grouping of countries awaiting news of their candidacy for EC membership, including Turkey and, in Eastern Europe, Slovakia, the Czech Republic, Hungary and Poland, aside from countries in EFTA such as Sweden. The EC therefore has yet to reach its maximum potential, both in size and in standardization and coordination of policies across the community.

Meanwhile, pressures continue to build outside the Community. Japan seeks leadership of the Pacific Rim and the United States continues to hold sway over the North American Free Trade

Table 3.1 Economic comparison of the Asian Economic Zone, the North American Free Trade Area and the European Community plus the European Free Trade Association, 1989 (in US dollars).

	Asia	NAFTA	EC and EFTA	World
Population (million)	1,620	360	358	5,206
GDP ($ trillion)	3,853	5,864	5,532	19,982
Exports ($ billion)	656	509	1,320	2,902
Imports ($ billion)	561	636	1,360	3,046

Source: *Globe and Mail*, Toronto, 24 September 1992.

Table 3.2 Selected economic indicators (1990 figures).

Country/region	Population (millions)	GNP (bn US$)	Exports (bn US$)
United States	251	5,391	371.5
Canada	27	535	125
Mexico	85	210	26.7
EC	328	6,010	526
Japan	124	2,942	287

Source: Brigitte Levy (1992), 'NAFTA: The competitiveness challenge', *Dimensions of International Business*, **8**, School of Business, Carleton University International Business Study Group, Ottawa, Canada, Fall, p. 45.

Agreement easily as the dominant partner, since Canada has only 27 million people and Mexico 85 million, but Mexico also has high poverty levels so these people could not be termed 'consumers' although it is hoped that they will be in the longer term. There are some very important differences to be drawn also in relation to the EC. First, in North America it is a free trade agreement, not a proposal for a customs union. The main features of NAFTA are the elimination of tariffs on trade in all goods by 1 January 1998; trade liberalization in services, and safeguards which still allow quantitative restrictions on agricultural goods as well as shipbuilding; the preservation of marketing boards and exemption for key sensitive areas in Canada such as culture, transportation, basic communications and breweries. Free trade is therefore expected to produce dislocation. In Asia, Japan, which is by far the strongest economic force in the region, continues to ally itself with the United States and remains aloof from the other Asian countries which look to Japan for economic leadership within the region.

There is a worldwide market for investment opportunities and, while China has captured a significant proportion of whatever Western foreign direct investment has been made in recent years, Eastern Europe is now beginning to recapture some lost ground here. This only reinforces the point that we live in a global economy with interdependencies greater than politicians would have us believe (except at election time). Political interventionism in trade constantly remains an issue to be faced. The Japanese model of industry-government relations has been tried in various Western markets and has failed. Brussels, seen as the seat of Euro-power and the location of faceless community-wide bureaucracy, is often a

Table 3.3 Main sources of the US deficit.

Japan	$54 billion
China	$24 billion
Taiwan	$10 billion
Germany	$9 billion
Canada	$7 billion

Source: Rob Norton (1993), 'Will tough talk mean trade wars?', *Fortune*, **127** (5), p. 93.

symbol of derision, the focus of hate, ignorance and grave misunderstanding by millions of Euro-consumers who can now be clearly discerned, with tastes in clothes, food and drink that cut across national borders with the emergence of new advertising media, including satellite television, which is ready to exploit this large, new, potential market. Politicians have the task of regulating for a level playing field, but it is up to companies to accept the challenge of whether or not they wish to play in this new environment which will require not only organizational change, but also cultural adaptation to new methods of operation, as the dislocation expected of free trade begins to bite. Trade deficits will, however, continue to colour relations between trading partners.

Checklist: be aware

Opportunity analysis – the what, where, how and when, which requires information:

- Size and structure of the market.
- Level and distribution of income and wealth.
- Assess competitive strengths and weaknesses.
- Niche opportunity (a small market segment large enough only for one company, but virtually unassailable).

Legal constraints – non-tariff barriers remain the largest single obstacle to free trade.

- Technological breakthrough can be held back by legal obstacles.
- Constraints regarding monopoly power will affect merger/acquisition.
- Constraints regarding pricing in terms of minimum prices, price floors or price ceilings (maximum price); recommended resale price maintenance.
- Employee legislation.
- Taxation and double taxation treaties.
- Boycotts or other constraints in force or pending.

Nationalistic sentiments giving rising to preferential policies:

- At national and local government level.
- At individual purchasing level.

Corporate size alone will not change traditional culture:

- Food remains the most culture-bound product, while fast food is an American export which is now global.
- Language still remains the most outward manifestation of culture which can often be very revealing. The Inuit of northern Canada may have many different words and expressions for cold and snow, but the same applies in Scotland when describing rain!

Public relations, publicity and lobbying can be very effective:

- At the European Community level.
- At national government level.
- At provincial or city council level.

References and further reading

Brockhouse, Gordon (1992), 'A phone call that does it all', *Canadian Business*, December, pp. 98–103

Brown, Donna (1990), 'Game-winning strategies for Europe's new market', *Management Review*, May, pp. 10–15

'Clout! More and more, retail giants rule the marketplace', *Business Week*, 21 December 1992, pp. 66–73

Department of Trade and Industry (1993), *The Single Market: A guide to public purchasing*, London

'The global economy: Who gets hurt?', *Business Week*, 10 August 1992, pp. 48–53

Leontiades, Jim (1990), 'Market share and corporate strategy in international industries', *Journal of Business Strategy*, 5 (1), pp. 30–7

Levy, Brigitte (1992), 'NAFTA: The competitiveness challenge', *Dimensions of International Business*, 8, School of Business, Carleton University International Business Study Group, Ottawa, Canada, Fall, p. 45

Norton, Rob (1993), 'Will tough talk mean trade wars?', *Fortune*, 127 (5), pp. 93–7

Onkvisit, Sak and John J. Shaw (1988), 'Marketing barriers in international trade', *Business Horizons*, May–June, pp. 64–72

Ramsbotham, General Sir David (1993), 'Marching as to work', *Professional Manager*, March, pp. 10–12

Rice, Faye (1992), 'What intelligent consumers want', *Fortune*, 28 December, pp. 56–60

Ryans, John K. Jr and Pradeep A. Rau (1990), *Marketing Strategies for the New Europe: A North American perspective on 1992*, American Marketing Association: Chicago, IL

Sprout, Alison L. (1992), 'Products of the years', *Fortune*, 28 December, pp. 64–9

Studemann, Frederick (1992), 'Serious about Skoda', *International Management*, March, pp. 46–9

'That's upbeat not beat-up', *Business Week*, 21 December 1992, p. 40

'When the state picks winners', *The Economist*, 9 January 1993, pp. 13–14

'Why Brussels sprouts', *The Economist*, 26 December 1992, pp. 70–2

4

Product/service

Anywhere you see our name is home.

Visa advertisement, 1980

Global products are few and far between and are found to be traded mainly in the Western hemisphere where the bulk of global wealth, but not the bulk of global population, is to be found. Wealthy nations tend to trade mainly amongst themselves, and companies are forever looking to increase the levels of value-added in their product or market offering. This fuels an irreversible trend in product design, although not necessarily in place of manufacture as, increasingly, it is the less developed countries with their low levels of wages and their free ports which account for an ever-growing share of manufactures for the developed economies, almost like offshore manufacturing plants.

Technology has forced a major change in terms of the availability of products and communications, and hence in our understanding not just of products, but of particular brands. Education is a good example of a service that has traditionally been provided on the basis that it has to be served directly to the client. This meant that it had to offer local representation wherever it was sought. Education did not travel; only trainers did. Technology has changed all that. Multimedia opportunities make it possible to enrol for MBA courses with the Open University in Britain, to listen to audiotapes, to watch videotapes, to tune into BBC radio and watch Open University television programmes. Henley Management College in Britain and

Syracuse University in New York offer a slightly different variation on open learning through home-based computer access via telephone modem, which then allows students not just to communicate with their professors, but to obtain help and advice from administrative services and to chat on-line with fellow students internationally.

Likewise, the assimilation of technology is brought to us as consumers through a wide array of media services such as television, radio and the printed press. Included in this, too, are telephones which link family and friends, sometimes via satellite, across the same country, and computers and fax machines which have the ability to handle large amounts of information very quickly.

Maslow's (1954) 'hierarchy of needs' is a good place to start to consider wants and needs, but advertising today is not so much about needs that could be filled with generic products, than about creating demand for brands. Physiological needs can be filled in a wide number of ways, but self-actualization will arrive only once we have gone beyond all the other needs to dream satisfaction and, at this level particularly, brands become all-important. Companies in Europe often give managers a car as part of their remuneration package, but managers relate to one another in terms of the size or brand model of their particular car. Identification of a car model with a particular level of management is a common thing. Some car manufacturers benefit particularly from up-market executive associations with their product, and BMW is an excellent example in this regard. Internationally it is seen as a luxury car that is capable of seating the family but can also appeal to the youngster in all executives since it is also uncompromisingly 'sporty' in terms of engine size, performance and general image. Exclusivity also plays an important part.

Bland products for a global market?

Few products transfer across markets as well as BMW cars, which appeal to essentially the same market segment across countries. Other manufacturers may just appeal on price or may find themselves stuck somewhere in the middle of the market as, for example, Renault, which has quite different advertising appeals in France and the United Kingdom for the same car, the Renault 5. The product may be the same, but the characteristics of the market or the profile

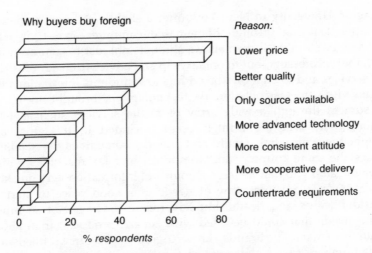

Figure 4.1   Reasons for offshore purchases. (Source: Edward W. Davis, 1992, 'Global outsourcing: Have US managers thrown the baby out with the bathwater?', *Business Horizons*, July–August, pp. 58–65. Reprinted from *Business Horizons*, July–August 1992. © Copyright 1992 by the Foundation for the School of Business at Indiana University. Used with permission.

of the target segment may demand some alterations. Consider the 'global products' that we hear so much about: name twelve. After the first few such as Pepsi-Cola or Coca-Cola, you are thinking more in terms of brands than standardized products. Kodak makes and sells film worldwide. Likewise, Sony and IBM manufacture and sell electronic goods and computers respectively. However, in the latter case, all manner of adaptations are required because of voltage, language (kanji or Cyrillic script) or interfaces between products. Usage conditions and the needs of the user also have to be taken into consideration. Also, the role of the buyer. We may be buying as consumers in our own right or as buyers or deciders in a buying situation on behalf of a corporation, in which case the dollar values involved in the buying decision increase significantly.

Standardization

Samiee and Roth (1992) conducted a study on the influence of global marketing standardization on performance, and what they have to say is very interesting. Conventional wisdom suggests that standardization brings cost savings which include economies of scale in research and development, purchasing, production and marketing, and the possibility of rationalizing international production and operating via exports. Standardization is also thought to offer more control over marketing programmes. What Samiee and Roth point out is that, despite many such claims being repeated over the years, few actual studies have been carried out. In their study, Samiee and Roth operationalized global standardization by using an index comprising five items:

1. Customer needs are standardized worldwide.
2. Product awareness and information exist worldwide.
3. Standardized product technology exists worldwide.
4. Competitors market a standardized product worldwide.
5. Standardized purchasing practices exist worldwide.

Global standardization was then examined against technology, product life cycle, marketing and strategy measures and business unit performance. Their findings do not support superior performance resulting from global standardization. They then go on to say:

> Common views about standardisation have rarely been supported empirically. It may well be that such views are based on a few casual observations. The fact that Coca-Cola and Colgate-Palmolive sell some of their products in more than 160 countries does not signify that they have adopted a high degree of standardisation for all of their products globally. Only three Coca-Cola brands are standardised and one of them, Sprite, has a different formulation in Japan. Some Colgate-Palmolive products are marketed in just a few countries. Axion paste dishwashing detergent, for example, was formulated for developing countries and La Croix Plus detergent was custom-made for the French market. Colgate toothpaste is marketed the same way globally, though its advanced Gum Protection Formula is used in only 27 nations. Perhaps brand names have the highest likelihood of becoming global, but the presence of a global brand implies a global position (i.e. the same position in every intermarket segment).

However, a recent article by Takashi Hisatomi (1991), a general manager in the product and marketing strategy office of Nissan

Table 4.1   The ten most recognized brands.

The World	United States	Europe	Japan
1. Coca-Cola	Coca-Cola	Coca-Cola	Sony
2. Sony	Campbell's	Sony	National
3. Mercedes-Benz	Disney	Mercedes-Benz	Mercedes-Benz
4. Kodak	Pepsi-Cola	BMW	Toyota
5. Disney	Kodak	Philips	Takashimaye
6. Nestlé	NBC	Volkswagen	Rolls-Royce
7. Toyota	Black & Decker	Adidas	Seiko
8. McDonald's	Kellogg's	Kodak	Matsushita
9. IBM	McDonald's	Nivea	Hitachi
10. Pepsi-Cola	Hershey's	Porsche	Suntory

Source: M. Strauss (1992), 'Cashing in on the clear Canadian image', *Globe and Mail*, Toronto, 13 March.

Motor Company, had some interesting things to say about Nissan and about convergence in consumer tastes across Europe, Japan and the United States, but noted that there are also certain specific demands within those markets that must be recognized. Nissan had passed through a series of stages in terms of its international marketing, for example:

1. Exporting automobiles as designed for the Japanese market.

2. Taking specific factors relating to the US and European markets into consideration, but designing and manufacturing mainly for the Japanese market, and exporting the product overseas. This resulted in shipments of vehicles that matched none of the markets.

3. Establishing from 1986 a 'lead-country' system, focusing on a target market and manufacturing a vehicle to match the needs and requirements of that market. This had led to successes with the 240SX and Maxima.

4. Currently developing a strategy on a global perspective, as Nissan now has production bases in twenty-one countries.

At the same time there is convergence in what the buying public is looking for in a car, at least in terms of size and styling. As Hisatomi states, until several years ago there was definitely a unique styling for each area. Recently, however, the Chevrolet Lumina of the United States, Peugeot 405 of France and the Honda Accord and

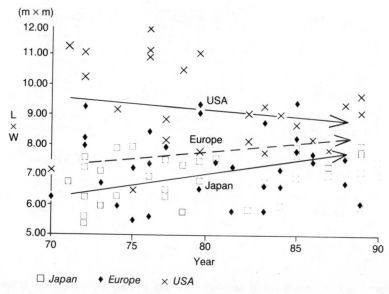

□ *Japan*   ♦ *Europe*   × *USA*

Figure 4.2 Consumer convergence on car body size across the United States, Europe and Japan. (Source: Takashi Hisatomi, 1991, 'Global marketing by the Nissan Motor Co. Ltd', *Marketing and Research Today*, **19** (1), pp. 56–62.)

Nissan Maxima of Japan have become similar in styling. Nevertheless, while similarities exist, account also has to be taken of some important structural market differences. This supports what was said before about building on similarities where these are to be found, while at the same time recognizing important fundamental differences.

Lennon (1991), in an article on developing brand strategies across borders, took this a stage further in citing the example of the Single European Market, saying that it is possible to see the management of brands across different countries as analogous to managing a brand through time in any one country.

Lennon's model for managing the global brand is described below. Over time the elements that make up the brand's personality have been formally or informally codified and passed down to succeeding brand managers and account executives. Over time the successful brand has developed a distinctive personality:

1. What the product is. Is it the same in each market or is it made to country specifications? What are the functional rewards?

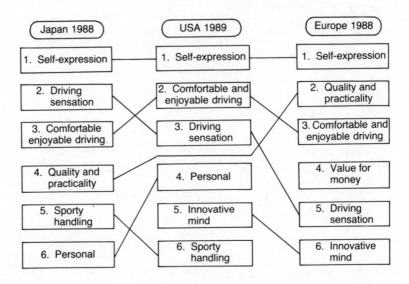

Figure 4.3 Comparison of consumer values of cars in Japan, the United States and Europe. (Source: Takashi Hisatomi, 1991, 'Global marketing by the Nissan Motor Co. Ltd', *Marketing and Research Today*, **19** (1), pp. 56–62.)

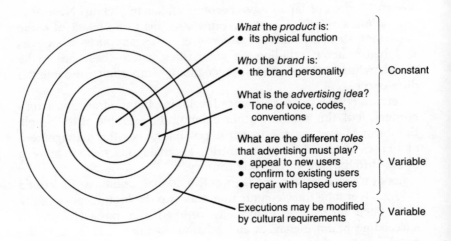

Figure 4.4 Lennon's model for managing global brands. (Source: Judie Lennon, 1991, 'Developing brand strategies across borders', *Marketing and Research Today*, **19** (3), pp. 160–9.)

Table 4.2 A standardized global strategy checklist.

	Yes Continue to explore	No Standardization not appropriate
1. Is there a global market segment for your product?	Yes	No
2. Are there synergies associated with a global strategy?	Yes	No
3. Are there no *external* constraints/ government regulation on ability to implement a global strategy?	Yes	No
4. Are there no *internal* constraints to implementing a global strategy?	Yes	No
If yes to all four, consider global.	Yes	No

Source: Susan P. Douglas and Yoram Wind (1987), 'The myth of globalisation', *Columbia Journal of World Business*, Winter, pp. 19–29. Copyright 1987. © *Columbia Journal of World Business*. Reprinted with permission.

2. What the brand is. If the brand was a person, how would it be described? What happens, then, when brand personalities cross borders?

3. What is the advertising idea that expresses the 'who' and the 'what'? All successful global brands have a set of rules, codes and conventions that dictate how they are to appear. Global recognition arises from uniformity in use of colour, logo, style of expression, music, advertising claim, etc.

4. What does the advertising have to do in strategic terms? What is the brand's current position in the market and how does it need to be changed? While executions will require different emphasis, the core personality remains the same.

5. What executional modifications are required to reflect cultural nuance?

Perhaps the best synthesis is achieved by Douglas and Wind (1987) writing on the 'myth of globalization' (see Table 4.2).

Adaptation

Rather than *resort* to adaptation, it is best to plan for it, otherwise you will run into it like a brick wall, and when you do, there will be no budget for corrective action! Instead of learning by doing, a more productive and much less expensive way is to anticipate the market. There is no substitute for market research and the intelligence it provides. It is a form of raw energy that you should tap into and harness to your needs. A basic understanding of the market is one thing; projected product potential is related but quite different. It requires assumptions of how the target market will respond to certain stimuli. This means doubling back to the point where the basic marketing question was first asked of the product in its domestic market, i.e. what need does it satisfy? Added to this is the question of whether market conditions are similar or not. In less developed Third World countries they will not be the same. Howard and Mayo (1988) projected how this kind of thinking would apply if we were to take the example of marketing Nestlé's baby milk powder in Africa (see Figure 4.5).

A quite different form of adaptation is provided by the example of the joint venture in 1989 of Philips NV of the Netherlands and Whirlpool of the United States. However, Philips, while willing to sell an interest in its major appliance business, was unwilling to sell its brand name. This posed the question of how business done under the Philips name could then be successfully transferred to another. Whirlpool decided to build upon its size, status and experience as the world's largest manufacturer of major appliances, and so the media campaign that followed concentrated on the strengths of synergy attained in this joint venture between Whirlpool and Philips. A successful public relations campaign in the trade media and in the European business and financial press resulted in some 180 stories in the European media, mostly praising Whirlpool for its move and explaining what Whirlpool brought to the branding equation. The message was continually reinforced that the value of the two parts, Whirlpool and Philips, was greater than their sum. Whirlpool was now building washing machines for the pan-European market, manufacturing in Naples, Italy, for sale in twenty-five countries.

To penetrate the trade, Whirlpool used a strategy of adding value, from special sales incentives to improved stocking and distribution of spare parts, to totally new products. For consumers there was the introduction of customer assistance telephone lines on Whirlpool's North American model, plus the possibility of dealer and consumer financing options through the parent company. Both the helplines and the financing were new to Europe. Direct branding with the Philips name was to continue only to 1999. It was decided that this

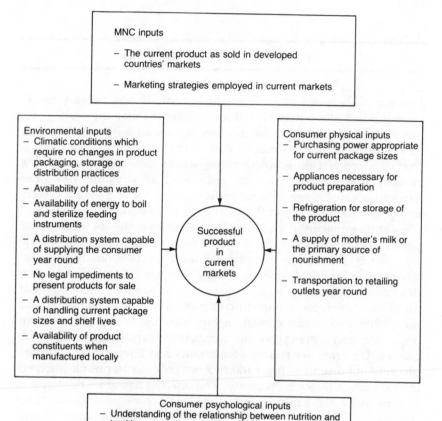

MNC inputs

– The current product as sold in developed countries' markets

– Marketing strategies employed in current markets

Environmental inputs
– Climatic conditions which require no changes in product packaging, storage or distribution practices
– Availability of clean water
– Availability of energy to boil and sterilize feeding instruments
– A distribution system capable of supplying the consumer year round
– No legal impediments to present products for sale
– A distribution system capable of handling current package sizes and shelf lives
– Availability of product constituents when manufactured locally

Successful product in current markets

Consumer physical inputs
– Purchasing power appropriate for current package sizes
– Appliances necessary for product preparation
– Refrigeration for storage of the product
– A supply of mother's milk or the primary source of nourishment
– Transportation to retailing outlets year round

Consumer psychological inputs
– Understanding of the relationship between nutrition and health
– Understanding of 'hard sell' marketing tactics
– Literate consumers able to understand written product usage instructions
– No sociocultural customs or taboos concerning the product or its proper usage

Figure 4.5 An application of the defence product management philosophy for Nestlé. (D. G. Howard and M. A. Mayo, 1988, 'Developing a defensive product management philosophy for Third World markets', *International Marketing Review*, **5** (1), pp. 31–40.)

would then be reviewed on a country-by-country basis as brand recognition for Whirlpool developed.

Local cultural interfaces

Differences between markets are important. It may be easy to get your product into a market, but the differences may then take over. For example, US product liability law is now a positive disincentive to export to the United States. Part of the material culture there is that, if a product does not work or, worse still, causes injury, the consumer will resort to legal redress. This situation has been brought about by generations suffering from poor product quality and poor dealer service at the local level – the customer interface. A US car manufacturer such as Ford sells cars to its dealer and provides dealer support. From there the dealer is responsible for the car. The customer may complain to the manufacturer, but will be stonewalled for it is seen as the dealer's responsibility. This situation has both increased the legal industry to the size that it is today and provided foreign car manufacturers such as the Japanese, who focus on quality and a caring relationship with the consumer, with an important and very powerful competitive advantage in the US market. US firms are run by accountants and lawyers, so there are plentiful opportunities for marketers not only to enter but to succeed in that market through creativity. The offering has to be right and it has to fulfil its promise, for the legal consequences of non-compliance can quickly turn a successful, profitable venture into deficit.

Society does not change quickly, so societal trends that become apparent have to be acted upon and integrated speedily into the overall marketing programme. However, it also has to remembered that society is composed of different groupings and sub-cultures, and homogeneity is not as widespread as many would have you believe once you move on from the basic necessities of life. Today, no matter where you live, a desire for food could be satisfied by a pizza, or perhaps a Greek doner kebab, or an Indian curry or samosa, or a Middle Eastern falafel or maybe just a McDonald's burger. The awareness already exists. What is changing is the way in which services are influencing our lives. To ensure standardization, companies such as Hilton or Sheraton impose controls that will

Celestial Seasonings/Perrier to market ready-to-drink tea
Celestial Seasonings Inc., a leading herbal tea maker, is planning to plunge into the $400 million market for ready-to-drink tea using domestic spring waters from Perrier Group of America Inc.

The first teas under the new licensing agreement will be available by July in California and the Northeast, officials of both companies said.

The teas will carry the Celestial Seasonings brand name but will be bottled and distributed under a licensing agreement with Perrier Group, probably with its Poland Springs, Calistoga, or Arrowhead brands of natural spring water.

The deal doesn't involve the Perrier brand, which is bottled in France and still trying to recover in the wake of the discovery that some of the water was contaminated.

The ready-to-drink tea category is shaping up as one of the beverage industry's hotter segments.

A week before the Celestial Seasonings announcement, the Coca-Cola Nestlé Refreshments Co. made a ready-to-drink iced version of the powdered Nestea, its first US beverage.

The Tampa, Fla.-based company was created almost a year ago by the world's biggest soft drink company, Coca-Cola Co., and the Swiss food giant Nestlé SA to market coffee, tea, and chocolate drinks.

Last December, Pepsi-Cola Co. announced it was starting a joint venture with the Thomas J. Lipton Co. to distribute Lipton teas and develop new tea-based beverages in the United States.

Lipton, which dominate the ready-to-drink tea category with an estimated 42 per cent share, previously had been distributed through a patchwork of soft drink bottlers, including some from Coca-Cola.

Analysts said that the alignment of Coca-Cola and Pepsi-Cola, the second biggest US soft drink company, with specific brands of teas almost assures more rapid growth in the category for the next few years.

'We are going to see a lot more action and a lot more money spent against the category,' said Hellen Berry, vice-president of marketing at Beverage Marketing Corp., which advises companies about various types of drinks including teas.

'Consumers are looking for more ready-to-drink alternatives to soft drinks,' she said. 'They are looking for healthy beverages or beverages that taste good. They are also looking for alternatives to alcohol of any kind.'

Celestial Seasonings, a privately held company based in Boulder, Colo., sells about fifty different varieties of herbal teas in tea bags. Herbal teas generally contain no caffeine.

Celestial CEO Mo Siegel said five or six varieties are being tested to see which would be best suited to being sold iced and ready to drink.

Source: 'Celestial Seasonings/Perrier to market ready-to-drink tea', *Marketing News*, American Marketing Association, Chicago, 17 February 1992 ensure compliance with their standards, making their hotels uniform internationally at the same time. However, the art of making a reservation, of paying for a hotel, of booking a rental car (another global product) and requesting a discount is another form of socialization of services that is affecting society across frontiers. Bank machines, the ATMs, are global and interact with banking systems worldwide. Retailers use electronic point-of-sale cash tills which accept credit cards from any bank worldwide. As consumer expectations have increased, the market potential for further products and services continues to spiral ever upwards, and for producers this becomes a search for 'low-cost excellence'. Robert C. Camp, manager of benchmarking competency at Xerox Corporation, Rochester, NY, has shown how this concept of benchmarking may be operationalized (1992). It requires, first, knowing the company operation and being able to assess its strengths and weaknesses accurately, knowing industry leaders and competitors and, finally, incorporating the best and gaining superiority by emulating the strengths of the best in the field and surpassing them (see Figure 4.6).

A well-educated society, ever more conscious of its rights and willing to assert them, is more wary of selecting amongst product offerings. Advertising alone is insufficient when there are consumer organizations and specialist magazines that provide benchmarking tests with competitive products. Value-added becomes the nature of the competitive response and quality is just one part of that, in so far as quality in this sense will be 'perceived' quality, as perceived

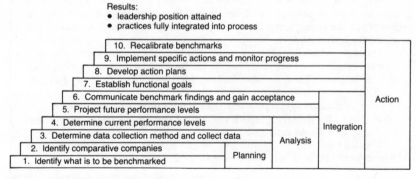

Figure 4.6 The benchmarking process. (Source: Robert C. Camp, 1992, 'Learning from the best leads to superior performance', *Journal of Business Strategy*, **13** (1), pp. 3–6 © 1992, *Journal of Business Strategy*, Faulkner and Gray Publishers, New York, NY. Reprinted with permission.)

by the consumer, and not 'objective' quality, i.e. the conformance simply to the manufacturer's standards. Some interesting points in this regard were made by a British professor of marketing, Stephen Parkinson, in his inaugural lecture at Bradford University, when he said that quality is remembered long after the price is forgotten and went on to explain the possible implications of quality as defined by engineers in terms of 'zero defects' (a term first used by US missile manufacturers!). In the United Kingdom, 99 per cent accuracy would mean the following:

- At least 200,000 wrong drug prescriptions each year.
- More than 30,000 newborn babies dropped by doctors or nurses each year.
- Unsafe drinking water for almost four days a year.
- No electricity, water or heat for fifteen minutes per day.
- No telephone or TV service for nearly fifteen minutes per day.
- Nine misspelled words on every page of a magazine.

Finally, he asks, would you be happy with a surgeon who could 'normally' find his way around your body?

Presumably, this enters into Maslow's hierarchy of needs at the safety level! Note, however, that this is at an industry level; it is not just one company or a named clinic specializing in a particular area. The point that this makes effectively, and it is one of which we are only subconsciously aware, is that the provision of utilities and services, particularly in healthcare, is generally very good. It is the absence of these expected standards that makes us complain. The advantage of branding is that it makes services much more identifiable so that, in Britain, we may talk of BUPA or PPP in terms of what they offer the individual in the way of private healthcare. This may be an interesting example from an international perspective because in Britain, unlike the United States, healthcare is a right, and free access is a cornerstone of the post-war welfare state. Today in Britain, as elsewhere in Europe, an ageing population is putting pressure on a cash-starved system, creating opportunities for medical insurance companies to enter the market with plans targeted at specific professional groups. It is an ill wind indeed.

Elsewhere, we have to make a judgement as to the receptiveness of the local market to the brand name and whether that product or service may be transferred wholesale or not. Kosaka (1992) equated standardization with effectiveness and adaptation with efficiency.

Checklist: be aware

After-sales service

This is the point at which your representation may be weakest: the ability to keep your products serviced and running in the foreign target market.

Branding

Is it descriptive of the product? Is it associative with the product? Memorable? Pronounceable? Does it stand alone? Does it tie in with company image? Is it registrable? Unique? Short? Does it say anything about the product? Is it appropriate? Does it sound sensible? Is it all persuasive? Is it modern and contemporary or old and biblical? Does it have close copies? Have these others already been registered? Then think again.

Default strategy

The worst possible scenario is to be coasting along with a product line and have your competitors shape your strategy for you.

Export product line

Initially, select a product appropriate for the market with a narrow focus, and plan ahead for new products.

Industrial property rights

What protection is there for trade names and patents? What legal redress is there in case of product piracy – counterfeiting?

Labelling

Important legal as well as cultural implications. Local language may be mandatory. If not, ignore, otherwise you may lose the premium effect of a quality imported product. Dual language may be necessary. Country of origin may be requested, as may listing of all ingredients.

Language

Still the area in which there is the greatest opportunity for humiliation, whether in brand name, packaging, advertising or accompanying product literature.

Legal

Product liability could be a real concern and source of company exposure, particularly in the United States. Distributor contracts providing exclusivity of sales area. Agency contracts and conditions for termination of same.

Local market conditions

The environment that you are to enter may affect how you do business. Conditions affect what you can do, never mind what you hope to do.

Local market expectations	May be incredibly high. Brand name may have been oversold in terms of service, durability of the product, etc.
Local product specifications	Ensure that local product specifications are being met.
Local suppliers	May buy goodwill, so determine possible sources of supply.
Measures	Metric or empirical measures.
Modification	Ensure that the product is sold only in the form as distributed by you and that the distributor does not alter, modify or change anything without prior written consent from you, the supplier.
Packaging	Is it the barrier property or the silent salesperson? Packaging can denote 'quality' or else 'no frills' value-added.
Pricing	Is there any particular value-added in the product offering (including accompanying service) which may fairly reflect a premium price?
Product quality variables	The eight dimensions of quality have to be rethought in terms of the foreign target market: performance, features, reliability, conformance, durability, serviceability, aesthetics and perceived quality.
Quality for customers as well as production	Implement quality control procedures not just for products, but for customer service as well.
Register company name(s) and brands	Ensure that you, as the manufacturer or exporter, register and hold title to all trademarks, names and patents, and disallow the distributor/agency from doing so.
Translation	Ensure that it is a quality translation. Always employ a local national to ensure comprehension. American companies have this problem in the United Kingdom and vice versa!
Warranty	This may be continent-wide, as with cars. Warranty periods are generally increasing and so is coverage, as product quality increases.

References and further reading

Camp, Robert C. (1992), 'Learning from the best leads to superior performance', *Journal of Business Strategy*, **13** (1), pp. 3–6

'Celestial Seasonings/Perrier to market ready-to-drink tea', *Marketing News*, American Marketing Association, Chicago, 17 February 1992

Chan, Allan K. K. (1990), 'Localisation in international branding: A preliminary investigation on Chinese names of foreign brands in Hong Kong', *International Journal of Advertising*, **9**, pp. 81–91

Davis, Edward W. (1992), 'Global outsourcing: Have US managers thrown the baby out with the bathwater?', *Business Horizons*, July–August, pp. 58–65

Douglas, Susan P. and Yoram Wind (1987), 'The myth of globalisation', *Columbia Journal of World Business*, Winter, pp. 19–29

Hisatomi, Takashi (1991), 'Global marketing by the Nissan Motor Co. Ltd', *Marketing and Research Today*, **19** (1), pp. 56–62

Howard, D. G. and M. A. Mayo (1988), 'Developing a defensive product management philosophy for Third World markets', *International Marketing Review*, **5** (1), pp. 31–40

Jain, Subhash C. (1989), 'Standardisation of international marketing strategy: Some research hypotheses', *Journal of Marketing*, **53**, January, pp. 70–9

Karel, Jan-Willum (1991), 'Brand strategy positions products worldwide', *Journal of Business Strategy*, May–June, pp. 16–19

Kashani, Kamran (1989), 'Beware the pitfalls of global marketing', *Harvard Business Review*, September–October, pp. 91–8

Keegan, Warren J., Richard R. Still and John J. Hill (1987), 'Transferability and adaptability of products and promotion themes in multinational marketing: MNC's in LDC's', *Journal of Global Marketing*, **1** (1/2), Fall/Winter, pp. 85–103

Koepfler, Edward R. (1989), 'Strategic options for global market players', *Journal of Business Strategy*, July–August, pp. 46–50

Kosaka, Hiroshi (1992), 'A global marketing strategy responding to national cultures', *Marketing and Research Today*, **20** (4), pp. 245–56

Kotler, Philip (1986), 'Megamarketing', *Harvard Business Review*, **64** (2), pp. 117–25

Lennon, Judie (1991), 'Developing brand strategies across borders', *Marketing and Research Today*, **19** (3), pp. 160–9

Maslow, A. H. (1954), *Motivation and Personality*, Harper and Brothers: New York

Papadopoulos, N., L. A. Heslop and G. Bamossy (1989), 'International competitiveness of American and Japanese products', *Dimensions of International Business*, **2**, School of Business, Carleton University, International Business Study Group, Ottawa

Parkinson, Stephen (1991), 'World class marketing: From lost empires to the image men', *Journal of Marketing Management*, 7, pp. 299–311

Samiee, Saeed and Kendall Roth (1992), 'The influence of global marketing standardisation on performance', *Journal of Marketing*, 56 (2), pp. 1–17

Strauss, M. (1992), 'Cashing in on the clear Canadian image', *Globe and Mail*, Toronto, 13 March

Walters, Peter G. P. and Brian Toyne (1989), 'Product modification and standardisation in international markets: Strategic options and facilitating policies', *Columbia Journal of World Business*, Winter, pp. 37–44

5

Promotion and publicity

Promotion is paid-for publicity using different forms such as personal selling, exhibitions, sales promotion (or point-of-sale material) and advertising, the one word which is sometimes used to subsume all forms of promotion. There is no country in the world that does not use some form of promotion, yet not all forms of promotion are to be found everywhere or to the same degree. Promotion may take different forms, of course, and again, there are different regulations prevailing in different parts of the world relating to what you can and cannot say and what products and services you can and cannot advertise. Promotion is, then, an umbrella term.

Some of these will be examined later in more detail. For the moment, let us stick with the issue of who the 'heavy' and the 'light' users of advertising and promotion are. From data reported in the *International Journal of Advertising* (1992), I have devised the bar chart in Figure 5.1.

However, what these figures do not reflect is that the promotional mix varies widely, especially once you leave the developed world for the Third World where a mix of cultural tradition, including religion, and low personal disposable income together with distribution bottlenecks hampers or totally excludes many forms of promotion. Literacy will affect newspapers and print media; personal disposable incomes will stymie efforts to launch television advertising campaigns; distribution bottlenecks and the inability to provide goods at point of sale will also exclude many other goods and dissuade their producers from advertising. The challenge is there, but must be met

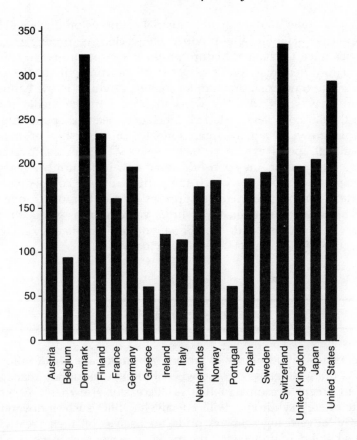

Figure 5.1 Total adspend: Europe, the United States and Japan (US$ per capita). (Source: adapted from M. Waterson, 1992, 'International advertising statistics', *International Journal of Advertising*, **11**, pp. 14–68.)

in different ways. For example, condoms may be advertised from a loudhailer in African towns on market days; in Britain, condoms may be recommended by a government anxious about the spread of AIDS, yet they remain banned from television advertising, along with haemorrhoid preparations.

Internationally, alcohol and tobacco are subject to the greatest number of restrictions (see Stewart, 1992), but it is the large number of other products that are banned by some countries and not by others that presents challenges to advertising agencies and their clients. Generally, in developed industrial countries products will be at the same stage in the product life cycle. As products age, strategies have to change. Mature products can be promoted using humour to differentiate one product from the competition. Restrictions, where they exist, are another matter. Products in the banned category may still find other ways to feature in the media from which they are officially excluded. One such means is sponsorship, which is growing rapidly internationally. Sponsorship of major international sports events virtually ensures that media coverage features the sponsor, the sponsor's name now being firmly attached to the sporting trophy for which the participants are competing. In cigarettes, Benson and Hedges supports tennis, Suntory supports golf. This strategy is open to all firms wishing to associate themselves with a sporting and, they hope, youthful and healthy image, irrespective of the products that they actually sell.

Transferability

This depends on a number of factors. An important organizational factor is the willingness or otherwise of foreign subsidiary management to accept a campaign that is successful elsewhere. A 'not-invented-here' syndrome will effectively stifle such innovation. Similarly, advertising agencies pride themselves on their creativity and their ability to understand the market like no other. Agencies do not like to receive such transfers as it means lower value work and the client actually telling the agency what to do next – ego would get in the way. The local subsidiary management and local advertising agency, either singly or in unison, stifle such transfers before they become serious topics for discussion. Sometimes, however, the transfer is achieved, as from the United States to the United Kingdom, but in the form of a US-made video which has been poorly converted from NTSC to the Pal/Secam system, and it shows. A grainy, badly defined picture shows only contempt for the intended target audience and implies that the company is just going through the motions, but not quite delivering the goods. In North American television advertising is spread across scores of television channels, whereas in the United Kingdom there are only four television channels to watch, unless you happen to subscribe to satellite television. Quality had better be good, or else.

Satellite television offers the greatest potential for wholesale transferability and the bypassing of national restrictions on advertising. However, for the individual consumer, initial set-up costs are high, decoders are expensive and planning permission is often required for a large disk to receive the satellite signal. With satellite television you can receive only one signal at a time, unless you have two decoders which is an additional expense. Even so, subscription fees are high and make the British television licence exceptionally good value. For reasons of cost alone, the market for satellite television will grow only within fixed limits and there are other factors to consider also, such as weather activity and its effect on reception. Nevertheless, satellite television will grow and we can expect to find many similarities in satellite-dish subscribers, particularly in this embryonic stage before the market develops. These are people who are affluent television addicts, so it offers a tremendous advertising potential across national boundaries. Radio Luxembourg was the first in international radio, and many of today's 'baby boomers' all across Europe were in fact weaned on this. However, it was fairly low-brow and unable to expand in terms of what it could offer. Today's youth market, which is internationally homogeneous, looks for the latest pop videos, not just the latest musical recordings. Consumer demands are changing and becoming more sophisticated, which drives the need for technology to meet this market demand.

Markets are changing also. The impetus driving the European Community towards the Single Market is creating, at the micro level, a great deal of the pressure for mergers, acquisitions and alliances. The Japanese, meanwhile, have failed to take advantage of opportunities existing for them to become global players in advertising, but that may be expected to change. Japan has generally reacted slowly to becoming a world player in trade and ancillary services. The yen is a lesser international currency than the US dollar; again, that may be expected to change over time, but over a longer period. The Japanese were slow to invest overseas but now have foreign direct investments in the Pacific Basin, Europe, North America and elsewhere. Services will follow production and therefore we may expect to see Japanese service multinationals on our own territory in future. It is a question only of time and inclination on their part.

Issues remain to be resolved. Grey Advertising's International Area Director for Europe cited the position in 1986 as follows:

1. Most readily globalized:
   (a) marketing strategy;

(b) product characteristics;
(c) product positioning.

2. May or may not be globalized:
(a) branding;
(b) packaging;
(c) advertising.

3. Almost always localized:
(a) consumer promotion;
(b) distribution;
(c) trade promotion.

There are few brands which operate on a worldwide scale. Kellogg's Corn Flakes is said to be represented on eighty national markets, but there are few other global brands where a standardized product is sold with the same brand name and internationally standardized advertising. Other things are changing, however, in that there are fewer, but larger, international advertising agencies and the advent of the Japanese is imminent. This will create further ripples because, while the average Western agency would feel uncomfortable handling the products of two arch-rivals, a company like Dentsu will hold accounts for a number of car companies. This difference in thinking, if reflected in attitude, can be expected to drive change even further. Finding a suitable focal theme around which to build an international campaign remains a problem, but the machinery to drive such a campaign is changing.

Kashani and Quelch (1990) proposed a framework for defining the source, level and nature of influence in promotional decisions, using three brand categories as a strategy point. 'Global' is where the headquarters' influence is greatest down through regional brands to local brands, as in Figure 5.2.

Kashani and Quelch question local autonomy in promotional decisions and believe that it is the role of headquarters to determine strategy. They see this question of standardization/adaptation in terms of a spectrum of opportunity encompassing a portfolio of brands, but note also that they suggest even for the most global brand that at least 50 per cent is devoted to local promotion and that a coordinator be appointed.

Actual transferability of the international campaign was studied by Vardar (1992), and she discovered what she called a 'Mirroring effect' (see Figure 5.3). This explained the organizational framework

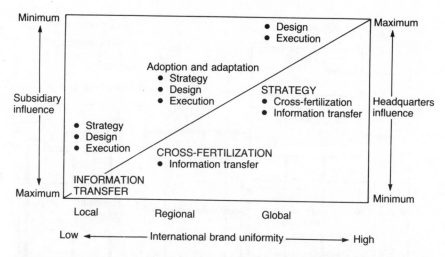

Figure 5.2 Influence and roles in international sales promotion. (Source: Kamran Kashani and John A. Quelch, 1990, 'Can sales promotion go global?', *Business Horizons*, May–June, pp. 37–43. Reprinted from *Business Horizons*, May–June 1990. © Copyright 1990 by the Foundation for the School of Business at Indiana University. Used with permission.)

within which the agency interacted with the client to develop or transfer campaigns to other markets.

Having said all this, a bold, brash, innovative idea can transfer across markets well. Like all other airlines, British Airways was severely hit by the record low travel levels caused by the Gulf War in 1991, but it responded by giving away 50,000 tickets in an international campaign costing $90 million. At the end of 1991, the

Table 5.1 Expected allocation of promotion expenditures according to a brand's geographical equity.

Brand type	Sales promotion expenditure mix		
	Local	Regional	Global
Local	100%		
Regional	75%	25%	
Global	50%	25%	25%

Source: Kamran Kashani and John A. Quelch (1990), 'Can sales promotion go global?', *Business Horizons*, May–June, pp. 37–43.

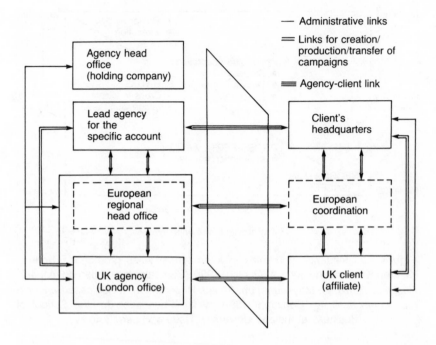

Figure 5.3 The mirroring effect: how agencies and clients organize themselves when conducting global advertising campaigns. (Source: Nukhet Vardar, 1992, *Global Advertising: Rhyme or reason?*, Paul Chapman: London.)

airline found itself with passenger figures only 4 per cent below the record year that they had had in 1990.

Why advertising cannot be standardized

1. Perceptions of consumer target groups:

    *   The attitudes of consumerists, students, academics and managers, about advertising across countries. The strongest differences exist between managers and consumerists, but no within-group differences emerge in regional sub-groups.[1]

    *   The similarities regarding cross-border consumers who have high incomes, a good education, white-collar work, interests in seeking information, low status concern, low conservatism and low dogmatism.[2]

- A strong reaffirmation that segmenting customers according to their needs across borders ignores the differences in 'symbolic references' that are crucial for the success of the advertising.[3]

2. Product groups:

    - Brands with simple advertising propositions, that have a low information content and that are low-involvement packaged goods, as well as products and services directly related to overseas travel or communications, are more suitable for global advertising.[4]

    - International advertising requires favourable conditions with regard to the availability of the product, competitive country climate, consumer usage segmentation, advertising history, the advertiser's organizational structure and the available advertising package.[5]

    - In the low-tech world of packaged goods, brands with an essentially functional appeal may be more successful in a global approach.[6]

    - World brands benefit from standardized advertising if they are ubiquitous and universal in appeal, they are consumed for the same basic reasons, their similarities outweigh their differences and they have consistent and long-term positioning. They do not work in extreme cultural differences and in ethnic situations.[7]

    - E. Meyer, Chairman of Grey Advertising, is quoted as stating that high-tech products lend themselves more easily to globalization, and also that products with a nationalistic flavour can take advantage of global marketing opportunities if the specific country has a good reputation in the field.[8]

    - World products, such as Universal Medical Products' disposable syringes, go for bigger markets; these are very high-volume goods made at low cost to a single design for everyone. They are insensitive to differences in their users.[9]

    - Consumer non-durables, low-tech assembly companies, heavy raw material processing industries, wholesaling and service businesses are not suitable for global practices.[10]

    - Products that enjoy high economies of scale are not very culturally bound and are easier to market globally. Most packaged goods are less susceptible to economies of scale than durables. Younger people, frequent travellers and fashion followers generally use fewer culture-bound products.[11]

3. Market readiness:

    - An example is given where a product from Acorn was positioned differently in different campaigns in the United Kingdom, United States and West Germany, according to the product's stage in its life cycle.[12]

    - Apple is cited as an example of a company that had to use local strategies because computer preparedness was different in each country.[13]

4. Popular media in different countries:

   - An emphasis on the need to tailor media selection, even for different product groups.[14]

5. Differences in advertising messages:

   - An exploration into the differences between American and Swedish advertising with the help of Clio winners and cinema commercials in terms of the advertising strategies used as well as how inform-ative they are. Large differences are reported.[15]

   - A comparison of the information content of ads and their time of airing in Ecuador, the United States and Australia. The most informative ads were found in Ecuador, where there are more products in the introduction stages of their life cycles.[16]

   - A measurement of advertising effectiveness on US citizens, Thais in the United States, foreigners in the United States and Thais in Thailand. It is argued that different advertisements are needed for foreigners living in the United States. Examples are given from McDonald's, Coca-Cola and Kentucky Fried Chicken of advertising to blacks, to Hispanics and to women.[17]

   - The different interpretations of advertising motifs caused by differ-ent perceptions across countries. The differently accepted norms and regulations (for example, in Spain, Denmark and Holland, the wearing of the wedding ring on the right rather than the left hand).[18]

   - How can the positioning of a car be standardized as 'sporty' where there is a 70-mph speed limit?[19]

   - A comparative study of three product groups, examining US and Singaporean students' responses in their use of information sources. The findings indicate a lack of cultural differences in this respect, as both groups exhibited a heavy reliance on word-of-mouth advertising. This is one of the exceptions, where the findings do not show significant differences between two groups.[20]

6. Advertising styles and types:

   - Referring to E. Meyer's views, this study mentions ads with visual appeal that avoid the problems of translation. Brands promoted with image campaigns also travel well, where themes with a universal appeal are used, such as eroticism and wealth.[21]

   - Japanese ads are full of emotion and entertainment rather than being based on an understanding of others through guessing; this is also reflected in the advertising.[22]

   - A suggestion to use emotional approaches when advertising to prospective buyers, but the use of rational arguments when advertising to near-to-actual buyers.[23]

   - Retail advertising is emphasized as being more difficult to monitor by headquarters. The retail advertising technique requires local cultural knowledge.[24]

- A report that sales promotion agencies are finding it difficult to handle international promotions. Language differences, regulations and restrictions on the value of giveaways are cited as reasons for the problems faced.[25]

- Although *Sky* magazine was launched as a pan-European magazine, different sales promotions and techniques are used in different countries to increase its sales.[26]

Source: Nukhet Vardar (1992), *Global Advertising: Rhyme or reason?*, Paul Chapman: London.

Notes

1. J. R. Wells Jr and J. K. Ryans Jr (1982), 'Attitudes towards advertising: A multinational study', *Journal of International Business Studies*, **13** (3), Winter, pp. 121–9.
2. R. Martenson (1987), 'Is standardisation of marketing feasible in culture-bound industries? A European case study', *International Marketing Review*, Autumn, pp. 7–17.
3. G. Harris (1984) 'The globalisation of advertising', *International Journal of Advertising*, **3** (3), pp. 223–35.
4. *Idem.*
5. A. E. Pitcher (1985), 'The role of branding in international advertising', *International Journal of Advertising*, **4**, pp. 241–6.
6. R. Ritchie (1986), 'Global branding need not mean global advertising', *ADMAP*, January, pp. 39–42.
7. R. M. Diaz (1985), 'Advertising in foreign markets', *SAM Advanced Management Journal*, **50** (4), Autumn, pp. 12–20.
8. R. Fannin (1984), 'What agencies really think of global theory', *Marketing and Media Decisions*, **19** (15), pp. 74–82.
9. S. Braidwood (1984), 'World Products', *Design*, **429**, September, pp. 40–6.
10. T. Hout, M. E. Porter and E. Rudden (1982), 'How global companies win out', *Harvard Business Review*, September–October, **60**, pp. 98–108. (Harvard Reprint no. 82504)
11. J. A. Quelch and E. J. Hoff (1986), 'Customising global marketing', *Harvard Business Review*, **64** (3), May–June, pp. 59–69.
12. F. McEwan (1984), 'A dichotomy in campaign style', *The Financial Times*, 26 January, p. 14.
13. A. J. Rutigliano (1986), 'The debate goes on: Global versus local advertising', *Management Review*, **75** (6), pp. 27–31.
14. A. Summers (1986), 'Sustaining a multiproduct brand name', *ADMAP*, January, pp. 29–38.
15. R. Martenson (1987), 'Content in American and Swedish advertising', *International Journal of Advertising*, **6** (2), pp. 133–44.
16. W. Renforth and S. Raveed (1983), 'Consumer information cues in TV advertising: A cross-country analysis', *Journal of the Academy of Marketing Science*, **11** (3), Summer, pp. 216–25.
17. S. Onkvisit and J. J. Shaw (1984), 'Identifying marketing attributes necessary for standardised international advertising', *Mid-Atlantic Journal of Business*, **22** (1), Winter, pp. 43–57.
18. S. W. Dunn and A. W. Barban (1986), *Advertising: Its role in modern marketing*, 6th edn, CBS College Publishing: New York.
19. M. J. Gratia (1984), 'The European advertising of the Ford Sierra: A comparative study in Belgium, UK and Luxemburg', BSc dissertation, UMIST, Manchester.

20. C. T. Tan and J. J. Dolich (1983), 'A comparative study of consumer information seeking: Singapore versus U.S.', *Journal of the Academy of Marketing Science*, **11** (3), Summer, pp. 313–22.
21. R. Fannin (1984), 'What agencies really think of global theory', *Marketing and Media Decisions*, **19** (15), pp. 74–82.
22. M. Ishikawa (1987), 'Latest trends in Japanese advertising', paper presented at the 15th World Industrial Advertising Congress, Brussels.
23. L. Einar (1987), 'Working with advertising agencies', paper presented at the 15th World Industrial Advertising Congress, Brussels.
24. D. Berger (1986), 'Theory into practice: The FCB grid', *European Research*, **14** (1), pp. 35–46.
25. D. M. Peebles and J. K. Ryans Jr. (1984), *Management of International Advertising: A marketing approach*, Allyn and Bacon: Boston, MA.
26. D. Hall (1987), 'Learning the global language', *Marketing*, 19 February, pp. 40–1.

Origination costs for foreign markets

Creativity does not come cheap. What is effective and strikingly successful in one country may be perceived as offensive, lacklustre, boring or even confusing in another. Language plays a part, as do the use and meaning of colours and the significance that we attach to them. Symbols differ in meaning also; for example, the snake has a strong biblical connection with women and may therefore be an effective marketing tool, but if we use the snake as a symbol in a country where the people are used to eating them, the significance will be lost.

How quickly can we arrive at getting our message across? Increasingly companies appear to be moving away from product advertising to international advertising, moving the focus away from product quality to good corporate citizenship. Partly this is due to a social trend that enquires into the behaviour of industrial companies, particularly with worldwide awareness of pollution now at an all-time high. The other aspect of this is the need to standardize, and it is easier to standardize if you have a simple message – hence the trend now for oil companies, for example, to show what they are doing for society rather than overt advertising for their product line. However, such 'socially responsible' messages always end with the corporate logo to aid recall. Effectiveness is dependent upon the interaction of a number of variables:

1. Vehicle used to convey the message to the target audience.
2. Exposure to the target market by the means selected above.
3. Perceptions of those who have come in contact with the advertisement.
4. Communication and understanding. Comprehension of the intended message.
5. Feedback, ultimately through the sales loop although there may be significant time lags involved unless direct mail was being used. Direct mail has quickly usurped a place for itself in the promotional mix.

Table 5.2 Total expenditure on direct marketing by country (1990 in million ECUs).

Country	Mailings	Direct advertising	Telemarketing/ other	Total	ECU/ head	% of total
Germany	3,960	2,540	920	7,420	119	30
France	3,460	430	1,170	5,080	90	20
Italy	2,490	1,040	80	3,610	63	15
United Kingdom	1,320	1,930	120	3,370	59	14
Netherlands	1,010	240	1,000	2,250	150	9
Spain	440	1,080	40	1,560	40	6
Denmark	610	160	90	860	168	3
Belgium/Luxembourg	210	200	50	460	46	2
Portugal	20	60	10	90	8	–
Greece	20	60	10	90	8	–
Ireland	10	40	10	60	17	–
Total	13,550	7,780	3,500	24,850	768	99
% of total	55	31	14	100		

Source: Adam Baines (1992), *The Handbook of International Direct Marketing*, Kogan Page: London.

The importance of publicity and public relations

Publicity or public relations is often referred to as being 'free'. It is so, only in the sense that no charge is levied for mention of the company name or product/service by the media that choose to give it attention. Newspapers, television and radio feed upon the plentiful supply of news out there to report. Newsworthy features of new products, new services or exciting technological breakthroughs, large speculative investments, mergers or acquisitions may present the company with opportunities for publicity. However, the prevailing view of what is 'newsworthy' (and therefore gets reported) has to be that of the media, not the company. Consequently, most large companies engage the services of public relations personnel and may retain the services of a PR consultancy to advise on the presentation of the annual report, a share flotation or any other event which may have important consequences for the company. There is significant growth and corporate interest in this area internationally and it presents an opportunity for a company to take essentially the same strategy and drag it across several markets simultaneously. It is important to instil the right image in the minds of consumers; it helps to build reputations and develops corporate 'goodwill' which translates into a tangible form in terms of brand equity.

Anatomy of costly, false rumour

The rumour made sense to Early May, and she was alarmed. A flyer posted in her apartment building had warned against that inexpensive soda pop, the kind her daughter liked to buy.

For weeks, the story burned through Harlem like wildfire: low-priced brands of pop called Tropical Fantasy, A-Treat and Top Pop were made by the Ku Klux Klan with an ingredient to sterilize black men.

'My daughter used to buy those sodas and I told her, "Don't buy them no more",' said Early May, 62, who declined to give her last name. 'I came from Alabama. That's why I believe it.'

A block away down Malcolm X Boulevard, 17-year-old Tosh Williams repeated the rumour as he stood outside one of many small groceries dotting the Harlem neighbourhood that makes up Tropical Fantasy's hottest market.

'I heard people talking about it, and I went into a store and saw the sign,' Mr Williams said. 'It's cheap soda that makes you sterile.' If anyone buys it now, 'they're fools'.

This is a story about a rumour – how it nearly soured the success of a little pop company and how the company fought back and won. It's also about being black in the United States.

It begins in Brooklyn.

Brooklyn Bottling Co. was limping into bankruptcy in the mid-1980s, barely surviving on sales of seltzer, when Eric Miller inherited the firm his grandfather founded in 1937.

The 33-year-old scion of bottlers revived the family business with shrewd marketing. He brought back the old line of fruit-flavoured pop, added a few more and changed the name from Crown and Glory to

Tropical Fantasy. His strategy was to keep the price down, far below that of big-name competitors like Pepsi and Coca-Cola.

Tropical Fantasy sold well in corner groceries from Boston to North Carolina, but Mr Miller couldn't control the counter price. Pop was pop to shopkeepers, who charged up to 85 cents for what he intended to be a bargain. He solved the problem by printing the 49-cent price on the bottle cap. While he was at it, he increased the bottle size from 12 ounces to 20. The new packaging made its debut last 30 September. It was a smash.

'It just started selling, selling, selling,' Mr Miller said of those heady days.

Sales rose 50 per cent in 1990, to $12 million. Mr Miller projected sales of $15 million this year.

Optimism lasted seven good months. But then the rumour struck.

By all accounts, it began in April. At least that's when the first flyer was seen. It was 3 April, to be exact, in Harlem.

Mel Johnson remembers the day. His company, WAM Beverage Distributors, owns half the fleet of twenty-five trucks that distribute Tropical Fantasy.

The anonymous handbills were crudely printed. The grammar was flawed. They got the KKK's full name wrong.

'ATTENTION!!! ATTENTION!!! ATTENTION!!!' each handbill read. 'Please be advise (sic), Top Pop, and Tropical Fantasy, also A-Treat sodas are being manufactured by the Klu Klux Klan. Sodas contain stimulants to sterilize the black man, and who knows what else!!!!

'You have been warned,' it concluded. 'Please save the children.'

Three days later, the same flyer turned up in Brooklyn.

'Overnight, the thing mushroomed to no end,' Mr Johnson said. 'Outside school buildings and churches, we seen kids on the street, giving out these flyers.' The youngsters, when asked, said some guy paid them $5. What guy? They couldn't say.

The rumour flew and spread, and stuck wherever it went. It galloped over the Brooklyn Bridge to East New York, Bedford-Stuyvesant and Coney Island. 'One of my drivers went into the Coney Island section,' Mr Johnson said. 'A group of kids started throwing bottles at the truck yelling "Get out of here! You sterilize blacks!"'

It fanned out into Queens. It leaped westward over the Hudson River into New Jersey, where Mary Truesdale, in Englewood, heard her nephew say a couple of his friends weren't drinking the stuff.

Ms Truesdale came across an article in the newspaper debunking the rumour and gave it to her 7-year-old son, Brian, to take to school, where the teacher discussed it with the class.

And still the rumour passed from friend to friend, child to parent.

Rosemarie Mulero looks after truants at a school in Brooklyn's Bedford-Stuyvesant section. She's also the wife of a Brooklyn Bottling truck driver. One day in the school staff lounge, she overheard one black teacher warn another not to drink Tropical Fantasy.

Another day, as Ms Mulero was about to drink from a bottle of the soda, a girl about 14 walked into her office. 'She said, "Mrs Mulero, don't drink that soda" and I said "Why?" and she said, "You're going to get sterile." She said she saw it on the news.'

About twenty inquiries came in to the Food and Drug Administration, FDA spokesman Herman Janiger said. 'We didn't believe it, but we decided to investigate.'

Pop samples were checked for the presence of saltpeter (potassium nitrate, which lessens sexual performance). Investigators visited Brooklyn Bottling. They checked the warehouse, the raw materials area, the production line. Nothing unusual was found.

At Brooklyn Bottling, meanwhile, things went from worse to worse yet. Grocers couldn't move the pop. Some shoved unsold bottles to the back of their coolers; others stopped ordering it.

Top Pop, made by Premium Beverage Packers Inc. of Wyomissing, PA, and A-Treat, made in Allentown, PA, lost business, too. But they depended less on the New York market.

Mr Miller had the most to lose, and he was the angriest. A man proud that his company of 125 workers is staffed largely by minorities, who likes the idea of offering poorer consumers a good deal on pop, he saw the rumour as an absurd attack and set about to stop it.

He hired Robin Verges, a public relations consultant expert in black concerns. Her efforts paid off when New York Mayor David Dinkins, a black man, agreed to drink Tropical Fantasy on television.

The news media jumped on the story. The Ku Klux Klan came out with a disclaimer: 'The KKK is not in the bottling business,' Wizard James Farrands of Sanford, NC, told a weekly magazine. Editorials in the city's major and minority newspapers raised stern voices against believing hurtful nonsense. Brooklyn Bottling employees met with the PTA and church leaders.

And Brooklyn Bottling, as well as the maker of Top Pop, distributed its own flyers.

'Someone put up a stone wall. We didn't have dynamite, but we have a pick and we're breaking it down, stone by stone,' Mr Miller said. 'We just went around re-educating and shaming people. Step by step, people are realizing it's a hoax.'

He also bought a billboard truck to drive around affected areas touting Tropical Fantasy. As summer approached, he gave away free samples. Then he waited for the hot weather. What thirsty kid can resist a bargain?

A month later, stores were refilling their stocks. Taped to the smudged plexiglass that inner-city stores use to thwart pilferers, customers found photocopies of editorials and a letter from Mr Dinkins promising the pop was safe.

The wait worked.

'I'd say we got most of our consumers back,' Mr Miller could say by mid-June. 'But we had three months of horror.'

Like the other bottlers hit by the rumour, he believes a jealous competitor planted the story.

'Right now, the economy is so bad, the big boys are as nervous as the little boys,' he said. The rumour was 'racism for economics', he said. 'What's more frightening to blacks than the Klan and sterility? If they said I used cheap ingredients, would it concern them?'

Major bottlers deny involvement.

Mr Miller hired a detective agency to investigate, and the Kings County district attorney's office also looked into the case. But the agency quit after reaching only dead ends, and the DA's office came up with nothing.

Source: 'Anatomy of costly, false rumour', *Globe and Mail*, Toronto, 2 July 1991, pp. A1, A15

100%
true
total
immersion

minimum stay – one week
available 12 months a year

very intensive language learning program
originally designed for executives
in EEC member countries to learn the
languages of other EEC countries

suitable for senior level management/CEOs

live and study in the home of
a language teacher, not in a school

excellent for improving proficiency
in a limited amount of time

___

no contact with people who speak
your language

___

france · spain · italy
portugal · germany · holland
argentina · taiwan · russia
united states · canada
england · ireland · scotland

to be added in the future:
sweden · mexico · costa rica · japan

also, for your convenience:

Los Angeles
213/623-6911

San Francisco
415/391-7517

Miami
305/577-0232

International

Homestays
Box 5409, GCS
New York, NY 10163

Phone: 212/662-1090
Fax: 212/316-2095

Figure 5.4 Advertising language programmes. (Source: 'The report on international commerce in Florida, the Southeast and the Americas', *International Business Chronicle*, Miami, Florida, 14–27 October 1991, p. 2.)

Checklist: be aware

Advertising importance	Varies across countries. Even where levels of advertising are similar there are differences, due to humour and what is regarded as funny; language even in English-speaking countries; cultural and social norms including religion and literacy levels, and differences also regarding spatial distance and time.
Advertising restrictions	Most often voluntary restrictions; a case of self-regulation. Check for what is allowable and/or prohibited.
Collaborative support	What support is expected of the manufacturer/exporter in the target foreign market distribution channel?
Database marketing	On the increase, but there is a consumer backlash to 'junk mail'. A good database would be targeting goods and services at individuals interested in them.
Direct mail	Low levels in Europe, but high in North America.
Distribution	Will limit success of advertising if availability of product not guaranteed.
Global brands	Assume global positioning. Few and far between.
Legal constraints: watch for them	The 'picturephone' is now a product that is available in the United States. This will create new telephone selling techniques in the same way as the introduction of fax machines meant random fax advertisements being broadcast to all users.
Literacy levels	Affect print media campaigns. Produce sales literature, brochures, catalogues, etc. in the local language.
Measuring effectiveness internationally	Seek to measure effectiveness. New methods are being proposed and ESOMAR (European Society for Opinion and Marketing Research) is at the forefront of this harmonization.
Names	Test names for brands in local language. Also all advertising copy if you intend to translate it rather than create new copy.
National adspend	Varies between countries and within the mix.
Packaging	Packaging and labelling have to take account of local laws and requirements.
Publicity/ public relations	Extremely important area of operations. Vital to maximize exposure to free media publicity on, it is to be hoped, a positive image of innovativeness or of being a good corporate citizen.

Rumour	The most difficult problem a marketer faces. It is most difficult to undo the effects of a rumour mill and re-educate consumers.
Satellite television	A new means to circumvent national restrictions in future. With satellites being used for telecommunications, the global village has arrived. Check out the footprint of satellite television broadcasting and any constraints on advertising in countries receiving the signals.
Semiotics	Science of interpreting cultural signs and symbols. Watch what you use in your international advertising and how you use it.
Simple message	Most effective vehicle for international standardization.
Sponsorship	Popular way to ensure media attention, particularly of a product in the generally prohibited category, e.g. alcohol and tobacco.
Telemarketing	Associated with television direct selling, but telemarketing is telephone selling and often uses computers to call numbers with recorded messages.
Trade shows	National shows not only attract buyers, but local suppliers as well. Provide an opportunity to reconnoitre the market.
Transferability constraints	(a) Internal corporate management resistance. (b) Advertising agency resistance. (c) Target market cultural resistance.
Word of mouth	The most effective form of advertising.

References and further reading

'Anatomy of costly, false rumour', *Globe and Mail*, Toronto, 2 July 1991, pp. A1, A15

Baines, Adam (1992), *The Handbook of International Direct Marketing*, Kogan Page: London

Britt, Stuart Henderson (1969), 'Are so-called successful advertising campaigns really successful?', *Journal of Advertising Research*, 9, June, pp. 3–9

Caulkin, Simon (1990), 'Last of the ad-venturers', *Management Today*, February, pp. 54–8

Higgins, S. and J. Ryans (1991), 'EC-1992 and international advertising agencies', *International Journal of Advertising*, 10 (4), pp. 293–8

Kanso, Ali (1991), 'The use of advertising agencies for foreign markets: Decentralised decisions and localised approaches?', *International Journal of Advertising*, **10** (2), pp. 129–36

Kashani, Kamran and John A. Quelch (1990), 'Can sales promotion go global?', *Business Horizons*, May–June, pp. 37–43

Killough, James (1978), 'Improved pay-offs from transnational advertising', *Harvard Business Review*, July–August, pp. 102–10

Mueller, Barbara (1991), 'An analysis of information content in standardised vs specialised multinational advertisements', *Journal of International Business Studies*, **22** (1), pp. 23–39

Rau, Jane (1992), 'A gift for publicity', *Asian Business*, **28** (4), pp. 48–9

'The report on international commerce in Florida, the Southeast and the Americas', *International Business Chronicle*, Miami, Florida, 14–27 October 1991, p. 2

Rutigliano, Anthony J. (1986), 'The debate goes on: Global vs local advertising', *Management Review*, **75** (6), pp. 27–31

Ryans, John K. Jr and David G. Ratz (1987), 'Advertising standardisation', *International Journal of Advertising*, **6**, pp. 145–58

Samiee, Saeed and Kendall Roth (1992), 'The influence of global marketing standardisation on performance', *Journal of Marketing*, **56** (2), pp. 1–17

Schwoerer, Juergen (1987), 'Measuring advertising effectiveness: Emergence of an international standard?', *European Research*, **15** (1), pp. 40–51

Srivam, V. and P. Gopalakrishna (1991), 'Can advertising be standardised among similar countries? A cluster-based analysis', *International Journal of Advertising*, **10** (2), pp. 137–49

Stewart, Michael J. (1992), 'Tobacco consumption and advertising restrictions', *International Journal of Advertising*, **11** (2), pp. 97–118

Toop, Alan (1992), *European Sales Promotion: Great campaigns in action*, Kogan Page: London

Vardar, Nukhet (1992), *Global Advertising: Rhyme or reason?*, Paul Chapman: London

Vardar, N. and S. Paliwoda (1993), 'Successful international advertising campaign and the "mirroring effect" between MNCs and their agencies', *Journal of Euromarketing*, **2** (4), pp. 45–66

Waterson, M. (1992), 'International advertising statistics', *International Journal of Advertising*, **11**, pp. 14–68

Webb, Victor (1991), 'Media and cultural diversity in the Gulf countries', *Middle East Executive Reports*, **14** (5), pp. 10–12

6

Pricing

Bringing the product/service to the foreign market

To the consumer, this is the price at which the product is available and sold on the store shelves. To the producer, this price has to represent a fair return so as to maintain sufficiently high discount levels and rates of support for all the intermediaries in the distribution channel, from importer, if different, to wholesaler and retailer. Add to this uncertainties over foreign exchange, political controls over pricing, problems of parallel exporting and importing and problems related to payment that may include countertrade, and the magnitude of the pricing problem in the international context becomes clearer.

From customer sensitivity through distribution channel acceptability to standards of political acceptability (which may monitor for 'dumping' or unfair trade subsidies), the situation is indeed complex and offers the company enough rope to hang itself many times over. Pricing cannot be entirely standardized internationally for a number of good reasons, including foreign currency value fluctuations, political pricing controls and extant legislation in the target market which, to take an example, may give protection to branded pharmaceuticals for only a short period of time. Canada in fact offers protection to branded pharmaceuticals for six years, as opposed to sixteen in Britain. A political change in Canada to increase this level

of protection to twenty years will wipe out the generic phar-
maceutical manufacturing industry. The benefits of the action for the
patent-holder are obvious, but it is going to be difficult for the
nation-state to ask its citizens to pay higher prices now than
previously, although it is to be hoped that companies would then
take the view that they have twenty years rather than six in which to
recover their costs of research and development and thus spread
their costs more evenly over a longer time frame. There are a
number of variables to be factored into the foreign pricing decision
including variable costs (for mature products some of the fixed costs
may actually be 'sunk' costs which related to the original R&D and
have since been recovered) relating to the foreign market and its
methods of doing business. Market demand, inflation and competitors' prices can be foreseen, but suppose there is a new law on
corporate environmentalism which passes the obligation to dispose
safely of packaging back to the manufacturer? It may sound
ridiculous but it is happening in Germany, one of the three most
important markets in world trade. Leszinski (1992) has pointed to
the pricing minefields of the European Community where, on
average, a 1 per cent price increase results in a 12 per cent
improvement in a company's operating margin. This is four times as
powerful as a 1 per cent increase in its volume, but a price decrease
of 5–10 per cent will eliminate most companies' profits, hence the
implicit danger of the Single European Market where price differen-
tials range from 20 to 40 per cent and more. Price harmonization will
need planning and the time is now.

Additional foreign costs

Costs may be similar, but not identical. There are export costs (see
Table 6.1), although the actual costs may be lessened due to lower
inflation, stable exchange rates and growth in that foreign market, in
which case the exporter will be pleased to accept payment in the
foreign currency. Overheads come in when it is necessary to start
thinking about other things such as 'hedging': in other words, a
choice between gambling on the daily 'spot' market rate for dinars in
six months' time or else perhaps factoring the export debt now with
a forward rate of exchange built into the price quotation. For
importers, the same is available; they can choose whether to pay at

Table 6.1 Bringing goods to market.

	Domestic sale	Export sale
Factory price	$7.50	$7.50
Domestic freight	.70	.70
	8.20	8.20
Export documentation		.50
		8.70
Ocean freight and insurance		1.20
		9.90
Import duty (12% on landed cost)		1.19
		11.09
Wholesaler mark-up (15%)	1.23	
	9.43	
Importer/distributor mark-up (22%)		2.44
		13.53
Retail mark-up (50%)	4.72	6.77
	14.15	20.30
Final consumer price	$14.15	$20.30

Source: US Department of Commerce (1990), *A Basic Guide to Exporting*, NTC: Lincolnwood, IL.

the rate of exchange on the day that payment is due or else plan ahead and settle a contract with their bank now for delivery of a fixed amount of dinars at a future date, but at an exchange rate that can be determined now and so used in calculations of the export contract price in the national currency. This is known as 'hedging'; the alternative is currency speculation, where you may or may not find yourself with an adequate supply of dinars if there has been currency fluctuation between the time when the contract was signed and now, when payment is due for the goods that have been delivered. Price quotation terms can have serious effects, and the latest *INCOTERMS 1990* lists the latest revision of these terms which are internationally used, so as to incorporate necessary changes for computerization as well as changes in distribution systems and materials handling.

Another complication, of course, enters when payment is being sought in countertrade. This may or may not include the need for a specialist countertrade intermediary. It lengthens the negotiation process and creates complications for the buyer now eager to ensure payment at agreed terms, but through the exchange of a commodity of which he or she knows little. Countertrade used to be popularly termed 'barter', but this is a misnomer. Barter is payment for goods with goods. Countertrade is the proper generic term for trade exchanges comprising part payment in convertible currency and part payment in goods, but it has a number of variants which cover possibilities such as whether the countertrade goods are restricted in range or not, the percentage that they account for in terms of the final sales contract, the degree to which these goods are commodities (and therefore more tradeable) or manufactures (which can be sold only at a heavy discount because of the lack of spares and the after-sales service that can be offered to the buyer). Countertrade is greatly disliked by banks and by international institutions such as the IMF, but it makes trade possible where otherwise it would not happen. All countries in the world now engage in countertrading to some degree and it is to be found particularly in high-value, high-technology industries such as aerospace and computers.

Palia (1990) estimates that there are 93 organizations providing countertrade services. These organizations have 93 headquarters and 22 branch offices located in 62 cities throughout 27 countries. They offer 4 categories of service, handle 6 categories of product, cover 8 regions of the world and service 13 categories of client. Palia's analysis was based on 1988 data, however. Countertrade deals are usually shrouded in secrecy so it becomes difficult to analyze these contracts in minute detail. However, certain characteristics may be noted. It is a second-best alternative to hard convertible currency and will never replace it. Countertrade also involves the seller in long-term deals, so there has to be some commitment to that particular market in agreeing to a countertrade payment option, over which time flows of goods may be adjusted. For the seller it poses ongoing problems beyond the sales contract now concluded with the foreign buyer. It may, for example, have committed the seller to using local sources of supply whenever possible. Now, to defray the costs of an aircraft by offering navigational equipment, so-called 'avionics', the seller is committed to volumes that can only be spread over all of his or her production. In this way it can usurp the seller's existing traditional suppliers and can create quite severe dislocational factors. Beyond the supply of equipment, suppliers are also often included in the research and development effort of new aircraft models. In this case, the traditional suppliers will be permanently replaced for the duration at least of that particular aircraft design now being put out to tender. Price alone will not win back orders to previous suppliers as other factors, such as regularity and quality of supply, inspection procedures and just-in-time deliveries, may be more important.

Recovering funds from abroad

Segmentation studies may reveal a sizeable profitable segment in the target market that can be accessed by similar media to one's own market and for a product requiring little or no modification from the country of origin. This is a highly cost-advantageous situation when it arises. The problem is with the mistakes which the exporter then makes. For one thing, companies look at the country of destination rather than the company destination abroad. South America may be perceived as more 'risky' than the United States, but we are dealing here with perhaps only one company in each of these two countries. Credit status reports of prospective foreign clients can be obtained from banks through their respondent networks abroad. Also government trade departments often offer a similar service, and there may even be a similar service offered through the local chamber of commerce's international network. There is no excuse for not doing homework.

Assuming that credit is not a problem, difficulties in many forms can still arise over payment. Importers may claim immunity from liability resulting from government action which has prevented them from fulfilling their obligations. Equally, there may be one of those natural disasters termed 'acts of God' by insurance companies, such as a hurricane or tornado, which has wiped out an entire crop and made it impossible to fulfil a supply contract. 'Acts of God' are rare and conspicuous. Commercial reasons for non-fulfilment when one can retreat to a plea of *force majeure* are few and difficult to substantiate. This will resort to legal battles and possibly industrial arbitration.

However, it is also possible that payment is being made but cannot be withdrawn from the foreign country concerned. The government may decree, for example, that payment of all air fares must be accepted in domestic currency as well as foreign currency. This effectively transfers the problem of inconvertible currencies to the seller, who has then to consider the value of remaining in that market. From now on, massive reserves will be built up in that market with a high rise in domestic growth now that domestic currency payment is accepted. The problem for that foreign company in this situation is that it may be difficult to find any uses for those large domestic currency reserves as all outgoings have to be paid for in convertible currency.

Yet another possibility is legislation decreeing taxation on profits earned which was not even an issue when the foreign market was first being discussed. New forms of taxation can materially affect the profitability of a foreign venture. There is also a number of other threats, such as profit repatriation controls, exchange controls regulating the amount of money that can be taken out of the country, hyper-inflation and transfer pricing interventionism. Where companies are unable to withdraw actual profits, they then resort to such things as fees, commissions, repayment of company loans and royalties from the subsidiary back to the parent company. Inputs into the foreign market may be manipulated in price provided that they are still intra-corporate transfers, so there is the means at least to manipulate price so as to minimize tax exposure, creating, at least theoretically, losses in high-tax countries and huge surpluses in low tax countries. Inflation and foreign exchange stability also have to be taken into account, however.

Positioning for competitiveness

Companies may only be interested in the short term. For them, 'dumping' may be a feasible strategy, but it is one which almost always invites a political response. National competitive advantages extend to products such as Scotch whisky or even Perrier water, but examples in this category are few. Price remains a competitive tool and can be used effectively for positioning within that market. It may be desirable to attempt to carve out a market segment in the foreign market that is similar in practically all respects to the domestic market. Price can therefore be used to position the product (or service) at a certain market level. If it is a case of what the market will bear, or only what an affluent section of the market will bear, then it is a price-skimming strategy. The opposite of this is the high-volume/low-value penetration strategy used by companies such as Gillette and Bic with disposable products such as razors. The middle is a dangerous place to be in. This is where companies are simply following the market leader. This is dangerous because, if we accept what is said of the experience curve effect, i.e. that every time production doubles there will be cost savings of about one-third, then it becomes clear that the market leader has a cost structure that followers cannot match yet are being forced into accepting. This position is not well rationalized, but there are many in this category. At what segment is this brand aimed? Let us separate product class and brand. Brands are for unique, distinct segments of the market. They can be differentiated by means of price. At one end is the economy-priced brand and this may represent value. At the other end, price is used to connote quality and bring status and prestige to the owner of that brand. Luxury is a common association for these brands; so, too, is a message of achievement and attainment, as often used in advertising travel and entertainment or the credit card industry's 'gold' cards. Materialism, however, may not be as readily communicable as the brand's particular advantages, so it may be in promotion that certain changes are required.

Whether in a luxury segment or any other segment, competitiveness in world markets today requires an assurance of uniform and dependable quality from suppliers. Quality is not about luxury items; it is about all items produced with a manufacturer's brand name. The costs of quality, argues Crosby (1979), are free in that the costs of not getting it right first time are high. Measurement is against customer satisfaction, unlike days of old when quality used to mean conformance to manufacturer's specification, so quality was met whenever products fell within manufacturer's tolerance. Today it is recognized that quality cannot be inspected into a product. As to its costs, the further from the product line that defects are detected, the higher the costs of remedying the situation. Costs increase dramatically once a product leaves the factory and is found later to be defective. There is almost a geometric escalation in costs. Positioning can be enhanced by offering reliable brands. For foreign companies the benefits of getting it right first time are even greater as the costs are higher abroad than at home. Substitute value for price when thinking of your target consumer.

United Distillers, a major producer of Scotch whisky, is an example of a company that set out to understand the effect of price in its various markets in terms of market share and brand share. The most important finding was confirmation that market size is significantly affected by the ability of the consumers to afford the goods. This ability depends on how much money they have and how much they are asked to pay. Mature markets have a higher dependency on price than average. In countries where Scotch is still developing, income is comparatively more important. The study then moved ahead using an econometric approach.

Consumers used different brands for different purposes. Medium-priced brands were more likely to be mixed with something such as

How to be a Value Marketer

1. Offer products that perform. This is just the price of entry. Consumers have lost patience with shoddy goods and fashion will not distract them from flimsiness.

2. Give more than the consumer expects. Whether it is providing environmentally sound packaging or including air conditioning in a car's standard price, offering pleasant – and useful – surprises will win customer loyalty.

3. Give guarantees. Offering an enhanced warranty and ponying up full refunds when problems arise, can help justify that higher price.

4. Avoid unrealistic pricing. Compaq found that out: it hewed too long to premium pricing which its basic product could not justify.

5. Give the customer the facts. Use your advertising to provide the kind of detailed information today's sophisticated consumer demands.

6. Build relationships. Frequent buyer plans, 800 numbers and membership clubs can help bind the consumer to your product or service.

Source: 'Value marketing: Quality, service and fair pricing are the keys to selling in the 90's', *Business Week*, 11 November 1991, p. 133.

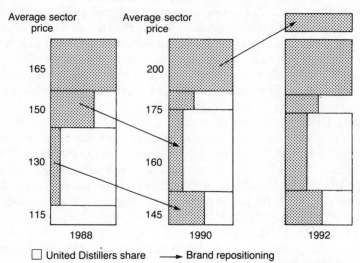

Figure 6.1 United Distillers: viewing country market 'Y' brand portfolio. (Source: C. Sims, A. Phillips and T. Richards, 1992, 'Developing a global pricing strategy', *Marketing and Research Today*, **20** (1), pp. 3–15.)

soda and were more sensitive to price. This left the cheap whisky brands and the deluxe brands and single malts. The study involved showing the same fixed set of brands to each respondent and this would test whether brands could be drawn into consumers' repertoires if their prices were reduced sufficiently. A salient set approach was used, representative of each respondent's current choice process, that would also reflect awareness and distribution of different brands. Although respondents saw only seven or eight brands, they were asked to compare across all existing brands. This led to the development of portfolio optimization. Figure 6.1 shows four distinct price sectors, and the share that the United Distillers portfolio had of each price segment. Price has been moving up steadily, but this shows that United Distillers was not competing in some sectors of the market. Some repositioning took place in the

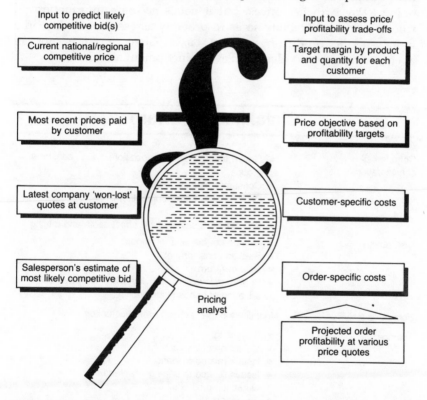

Figure 6.2 Information needed for price decisions. (Source: Robert A. Garda, 1991, 'Tactical pricing', *Journal of Business Strategy*, September– October. © 1991, *Journal of Business Strategy*, Faulkner and Gray Publishers, New York, NY. Reprinted with permission.)

lower-price sectors which led to a 10 per cent gain in volume share between 1988 and 1990 and translated into a 7 per cent value share. The second phase is to create a new sector by taking a brand from the top sector to create a new price category and further develop the brands in other sectors.

Tactical pricing, as opposed to strategic pricing, is transaction based. It can reveal significant economies in shifting attention to more profitable products, reducing competitive bids and gaining share with specific customers by cutting price where this will not lead to a price war, and exert upward pressure on industry prices in order to misdirect and confuse competitors. Three key components are price level, timing and method of communication. Tactical pricing is invisible to competitors, but also often to the company itself because of deals negotiated on list prices. It does entail risks in doing away with list prices, but it needs accurate information on true cost and profitability so as to properly assess profitability on a more specific product-by-product basis. Gross profit is not an adequate measure to identify real product potential.

Checklist: be aware

Commercial considerations	• Government, trade associations and consumer groups. • Consumer expectations. • Pricing behaviour of competitors. • Market trends. • INCOTERMS selected will affect costs and pricing.
Distribution	• Methods of dispatch of goods. • Sale on consignment. • Sale or return. • Proforma invoicing, i.e. invoicing for payment in advance of goods shipment.
Economic stability	Inflation/foreign exchange rate fluctuation.
Finance	• Budgeting. • Collection of invoices. • Issues related to loans. • Issues related to bank guarantees. • Quotation methods. • Countertrade. • Methods of payment.
Government	Attitudes of host and home governments to prices charged in host country relative to the home market.

Hedging	A contractual purchase of a stipulated sum of foreign currency for delivery at a fixed future date. This exchange rate may be discounted over the prevailing daily spot rate. It offers importers guaranteed prices from the bank and effectively eliminates exchange risks.
INCOTERMS 1990	The terminology of quotations changed significantly with the publication of *INCOTERMS 1990*. Watch the terms that you use and ensure that they are up to date and will therefore have the same meaning internationally. Cite *INCOTERMS 1990* as the source. In the event of difficulty, this could be important. The 1990 revision introduced some new terms and dropped others. Be sure you know what they mean and what you are quoting (see Appendix, page 96).
Legal constraints	As to what the government will allow, e.g. price controls, resale price maintenance, distribution agreements, competition policy, product quality laws and controls.
Local payments	Extraordinary payments. Bribery and corruption are despised worldwide but they exist and, in many countries, small bribes (known by a variety of different innocuous-sounding names) are part of the system where wages are low and the bureaucracy is heavy. It may mean making payments not just to one individual, but also to members of his or her 'extended family'.
Political constraints	Dumping; export subsidies; extraordinary payments.
Positioning	• Is pricing used to position the product in a certain way? • Demand elasticities? • Consumer perceptions and expectations?
Price escalation	A suitable clause allowing for price escalation is only sensible in countries where inflation is high and elsewhere whenever there is a large ongoing industrial project of some kind. Foreign project credit finance can be seriously threatened by cost overruns and inflation.
Security of payment	• Through credit check. • Accurate paperwork and documentation utilizing internationally agreed INCOTERMS. • Through pricing in one's domestic currency or using forward market rates for foreign currency through one's bank.
Segmentation	• Are there any possibilities for premium pricing? • Extension of product market segment across other national frontiers?

Standardization	How close or distant is this foreign market final price to the consumer from that prevailing in the domestic market?

Appendix: *INCOTERMS 1990*

The 1990 revision of INCOTERMS was required partly because of new transportation techniques such as containerization and use of multi-modal transport, but mainly because of the advent of EDI (electronic data interchange). A particular problem was where the seller had to present a negotiable transport document, notably the bill of lading which is frequently used for the purposes of selling the goods while they are being carried. With EDI it is important to ensure that buyers have the same position in law as they would with the traditional bill of lading. These terms are given in Table 6.2.

Table 6.2   Mode of transport and the appropriate INCOTERM 1990.

Any mode of transport including multi-modal	EXW	Ex works (. . . named place)
	FCA	Free carrier (. . . named place)
	CPT	Carriage paid to (. . . named place of destination)
	CIP	Carriage and insurance paid to (. . . named place of destination)
	DAF	Delivered at frontier (. . . named place)
	DDU	Delivered duty unpaid (. . . named place of destination)
	DDP	Delivered duty paid (. . . named place of destination)
Air transport	FCA	Free carrier (. . . named place)
Rail transport	FCA	Free carrier (. . . named place)
Sea and inland waterway transport	FAS	Free alongside ship (. . . named port of shipment)
	FOB	Free on board (. . . named port of shipment)
	CFR	Cost and freight (. . . named port of destination)
	CIF	Cost, insurance and freight (. . . named port of destination)
	DES	Delivered ex ship (. . . named port of destination)
	DEQ	Delivered ex quay (. . . named port of destination)

Source: *INCOTERMS 1990*, ICC Publication no. 460. Published in its official English version by the International Chamber of Commerce, Paris. Copyright © 1990 – International Chamber of Commerce (ICC). Available from ICC Publishing S.A., 38 Cours Albert 1er, 75008 Paris, France.

References and further reading

Crosby, Philip B. (1979), *Quality is Free*, McGraw-Hill: New York

Garda, Robert A. (1992), 'Tactical pricing', *McKinsey Quarterly*, **3**, pp. 75–85

Howells, Robert (1991), 'How to price products competitively in Europe', *Target Marketing*, **14** (5), pp. 32–4

INCOTERMS 1990, publication no. 460, ICC: Paris, France

Joelson, Mark R. and Roger C. Wilson (1992), 'An international dumping primer: Know the rules before an antidumping complaint arrives', *Journal of European Business*, **3** (4), pp. 53–5, 64

Kartbech-Olesen, Ruby (1989), 'World trade in cephalopods: A growing business', *International Trade Forum*, **25** (2), pp. 4–7, 30

Knetter, Michael M. (1989), 'Price discrimination by U.S. and German exporters', *American Economic Review*, **79** (1), pp. 198–210

Kublin, Michael (1990), 'A guide to export pricing', *Industrial Management*, **32** (3), pp. 29–32

Leszinski, Rolf (1992), 'Pricing for a single market', *McKinsey Quarterly*, **3**, pp. 86–94

Palia, Aspy P. (1990), 'Worldwide network of countertrade services', *Industrial Marketing Management*, **19**, pp. 69–76

Paliwoda, Stanley J. (1989), 'Countertrade', in Michael J. Thomas (ed.), *The Marketing Handbook*, 3rd edn, Gower Press: Aldershot

Roberts, Alan (1988), 'Setting export prices to sell competitively', *International Trade Forum*, **24** (3), pp. 10–13, 30–1

Sims, C., A. Phillips and T. Richards (1992), 'Developing a global pricing strategy', *Marketing and Research Today*, **20** (1), pp. 3–15

US Department of Commerce (1990), *A Basic Guide to Exporting*, NTC: Lincolnwood, IL

'Value marketing: Quality, service and fair pricing are the keys to selling in the 90's', *Business Week*, 11 November 1991, pp. 132–7

7

Place of sale/distribution

Moving goods from the factory to the foreign markets

While efficiencies may be gained in this movement of goods between place of production and place of sale, this chapter will focus on the place of sale. Logistics deals with this movement of goods and there is much to be considered here: goods handling, how and how many times the goods are handled, form of conveyance, transhipment, packing and time in transit. All of these factors bear heavily on this issue.

The cost of physical handling and goods movement is a cost not just in terms of freight; it also depends upon the duration time in transit, and repeated handling incurs costs due to spoilage (and therefore the need for better packing) and pilferage which may be found under a number of terms indicating waste and leakage. These costs must ultimately be reflected in the final price and so are included as such in Chapter 6. Particular attention must be drawn to the *INCOTERMS 1990* revision as the definitive terms for contractual use internationally.

In Britain at the moment, the only means by which goods can be conveyed direct to a foreign destination without transhipment is by air, but that will soon change when the Channel Tunnel opens for business and road and rail start to enjoy the ease and convenience of being able to convey direct to destinations without transhipment. Transhipment involves further goods handling and therefore delays, and includes the potential problem of goods spoilage and loss.

What the exporter is looking for is effective goods movement rather than handling and the conveyance of goods from factory to foreign destination. What has hitherto clouded this issue has been the INCOTERMS prior to their 1990 revision and the very traditional unchallenged process whereby a bill of lading would be sufficient proof that the bearer held title to the goods being conveyed. A bill of lading held a legal significance that an air waybill never enjoyed but now, with the advent of computerization, how do we stand with electronic signatures? These changes were long overdue and had to be incorporated. Everyone is better off for their arrival. The point to remember is not that international trade is changing, but that it has changed and decisively so.

How should you choose a forwarder?

It's true, the choices available to shippers involved in global markets are increasing. But the picture isn't all rosy. There are some risks. One way to minimize your risk is to screen your forwarders carefully.

What should you expect? Some forwarders well versed in global logistics offer the benefit of their experience:

- Probably first on everyone's list is to determine the asset liquidity of the forwarder. You're paying them to pay carriers and under agency law, you are still liable if they don't pay, says Lynn Fritz, chairman, Fritz Companies Inc.

- Check credit ratings and talk to steamship lines and carriers the forwarder does business with, advises Harold Stewart, The ICE Co.

- Fritz adds the ability and the top leadership of the forwarder to his list. Look at that the same way you would with any business partner.

- Ask forwarders their specialty, says Neil Mooney, Flagship Trade Services.

- Look for someone who has visited the destination country and speaks the language, adds Mooney.

- To be successful on a worldwide basis, a forwarder must have representation worldwide, continues Darrell Summers, The International Transport Assn (TITA).

- Personalized service is important, adds Louis DeMarco, chairman of TITA. The forwarder should be able to handle all shipping needs plus advise on packing, terms of sale, getting paid and negotiating letters of credit.

- An added service a forwarder with worldwide representation can offer, says DeMarco, is a check of the consignee. The foreign representative can provide information about the company and ask pertinent questions which could help avoid difficulties in getting paid.

- Forwarders should also be able to advise on general business practices and customs in the destination country.
- Look for expertise and knowledge at the port of export as well as the destination, say many of the forwarders.
- Other factors which might influence a decision would include EDI capability and levels of automation.

The result of the process is likely to be a mix of forwarders providing different types and levels of service. It is also likely to involve more or less direct involvement on your part. As Neil Mooney points out, if you have fewer boxes moving in Caribbean and Central American trade, concentrate your efforts with carriers where your volumes are, say, in the Far East. It takes as much time and effort to negotiate with a carrier on 10 boxes per month to Costa Rica as it does to negotiate on a 100 boxes per month to Asia. Let the forwarder operate where it is more efficient and remain aware of their activity. Get involved where your involvement is beneficial.

Source: Paul Murphy, James Daley and Douglas Dalenberg (1991), 'Forwarders are a vital link for shippers', *Transportation and Distribution*, August. p. 44.

Beyond arrival at the foreign port of entry there is a market yet to be accessed. Traditionally, books on this subject have started to plod through the advantages and disadvantages of the different market entry forms, discussed earlier in Chapter 2. Exporting via agent or distributor is immaterial to the foreign consumer who makes a value judgement on the product in question and the accompanying level of service afforded by the market entry mode selected by the producer.

Tangibles are how the product is received and perceived by the consumer. If the product was broken, how well did this company respond either in putting right the defect or exchanging the product? No other consideration matters to the consumer. What is real is what is available at street level. Global aspirations of the producer or metaphysical theories of internationalization offered by academics are worth nothing beside this. Customer focus is essential, no matter who your customers are or where they are located. The best possible mode relative to company resources means that there will never be a correct or best strategy, but that one must take a contingency approach of deciding the best mode for the set of circumstances. Neither is it a final decision that is being made, for, whatever choice is made, that particular mode of operation has to be vigorously assessed and monitored from inception to determine best value for both customer and company.

Comparing channels of distribution

There is a wide choice of possible alternatives: road, rail, water (inland and coastal), pipeline and air. What works for you is the only important consideration. Product, industry and distribution characteristics have a bearing on this, but to be effective, you often have to do something different from your competitors. Distribution provides many different means of doing exactly this. Note, however, that in the European Community it is actually illegal to have the same product bearing two brand names because of different distribution systems and hence two price structures.

Returning to the customer, the final consumer of this export product in question, the issue is one of value-added. Value-added is what is offered by the members of the distribution channel in terms of service to the customer that will be appreciated and welcomed by the customer to the extent of recognizing its value in a premium price. The product life cycle has an important effect here. When new products enter the market, it is part of the task of members of the distribution channel to educate and inform and, later, to point out the respective merits of one brand relative to another. However, as products mature, the buying public becomes more knowledgeable and a 'harder sell', so there is less need for information. At this stage, it is redundant and not appreciated as it was before. It therefore becomes part of overhead cost. All we need now is to sell the mature product on its characteristics rather than brand, and the public will buy. The last two years provide many examples of computer companies moving into direct sale to the customer via 800-line telephone numbers. Why? The personal computer is still continuing to change in speed, size, features and peripherals including multi-media options, but it established certain industry-side specifications such as its central processor, whether 386 or 486, ram size and hard-disk memory capacity. These features enable us to draw up a specification without reference to a brand name.

Despite this, the pressure is on resellers to prove that they are adding value. What started as a high-margin product is now relatively low margin with prices continually falling, as there are too many producers worldwide chasing too few customers and technology is moving so fast as to render the latest product obsolete within six months of its launch. The personal computer has become a generic and many department stores sell their own package of a complete computer system with their own brand name on it. Even this, however, is changing in that store brand names are inappropriate on such merchandise. Basic operating functions are what differentiate computers rather than computer or even store brand names. Apart from IBM there are hundreds of names in the market offering essentially the same features for different prices because they all offer the customer a slightly different package of benefits. The confusion present in this market is one that allows standard generic features to predominate in product offerings and therefore price levied.

Penetrating the market may be the task of an agent or distributor, but even where one or other may be successful, the reseller may not be receiving the support necessary to promote an unknown foreign producer in the target market. A high level of inventory amongst resellers may be seen to be an early success of the distribution channel, but if it remains there in its virtual entirety months later, it means disaster for the company providing stock on a consignment sale-or-return basis.

It is also important to recognize, however, that perceptions need not and often do not match, so that if one were to speak to a manufacturer and then the agent, two perspectives would emerge. Moore (1991) undertook a study of UK manufacturers exporting to Germany and of their relationships with agents and distributors. He investigated these relationships from both sides. Table 7.1 deals with UK exporting manufacturers, Table 7.2 with West German agents.

Producer, intermediary and customer perceptions

A coherent message is heard when everyone sings the same song in unison. The need to act in unison and achieve standardization of service is difficult. Each member of the distribution channel will have their own expectations and when these are not even partly met, dissension ensues which may affect the harmony and longevity of representation in the foreign market. The term 'synergy' is often used which is sometimes represented as $2 + 2 = 5$. In other words, the sum of the parts is greater than the whole. There may be some argument to support this, but equally it must be noted that the

Table 7.1 UK exporting manufacturers: survey of relationship development states.

	Relationship development states				
	New (n = 19)	Growing (n = 45)	Troubled (n = 9)	Static (n = 13)	Declining (n = 5)
Sales trend over 3 years	Growing slowly but moving to static	Growing quickly	Static moving to declining	Static	Declining slowly/quickly
Annual sales (£'000s)	38	272	190	130	256
Future	Uncertain but moving towards working closer together	Working closer together	Ending the relationship	Working closer together	Working closer together but moving towards uncertainty
Satisfaction	Uncertain	Satisfied	Uncertain	Satisfied	Satisfied but moving to uncertain
Frequency of disagreements (conflict)	High	Moderate	High	Moderate	Least conflict
No. of years exporting to West Germany	11.3	19	16	19	20.4
No. of products marketed in West Germany	6	20	55	8	12
No. of visits to agents per year	3.2	2.8	2.7	2.9	2.4

Source: Richard A. Moore (1991), 'Relationship states in an international marketing channel', *European Journal of Marketing*, **25** (5), p. 54.

Table 7.2 West German agents and distributors: survey of relationship development states.

	Relationship development states				
	New (n = 23)	Growing (n = 53)	Troubled (n = 15)	Static (n = 34)	Declining (n = 23)
Sales trend over 3 years	Growing slowly but moving to static	Growing quickly	Static but moving to declining	Static	Declining slowly/quickly
Annual sales (£'000s)	264	561	144	412	305
Future	Thinking of working closer together	Thinking of working closer together	Uncertain but moving towards thinking of ending the relationship	Working closer together	Working closer together but moving towards uncertainty
Satisfaction	Uncertain, moving to satisfied	Uncertain, moving to satisfied	Uncertain, moving to dissatisfied	Uncertain to satisfied	Uncertain to satisfied
Frequency of disagreements (conflict)	Moderate	Moderate	High	Moderate	Moderate
Percentage of agent's business with the UK	55%	45%	13%	18%	10%
No. of UK principals	5.56	4.96	2.67	3.87	3.81
No. of other principals (not UK)	5.35	5.61	7.46	8.37	4.81
No. of visits by agent to UK principal (per year)	2	2.2	1.8	2.97	1.78

Source: Richard A. Moore (1991), 'Relationship states in an international marketing channel', *European Journal of Marketing*, **25** (5), p. 55.

converse is also true: that instead of pursuing 'value-added', you may be pursuing 'value-reduction'. A prime example is to be found in the Eastern Europe of pre-1989 when East Germany continued to make the Trabant car, bringing in the individual component parts that went to make up the two-stroke car legend that was the butt of so many jokes, but lost money with each unit sold. It is easy to point to Eastern Europe for such examples, but there are many similar ones to be found in 'sunset' industries in Western Europe and elsewhere, where tradition combined with 'no brain' political interventionism continues to produce 'Trabantism'.

If you restrict yourself to thinking that the foreign market is serviced simply because you offload goods with the agent at the docks, then perhaps you should take up gambling full-time and leave business to others. Exporting may be a new form of business to the company, but it is rare that the target market will not already have competitors for the product in question with well-established distribution channels. The very fact that we have a market *in situ* supports this. The market mechanism tells us of shortages or surpluses, but it is market research or, more accurately, consumer

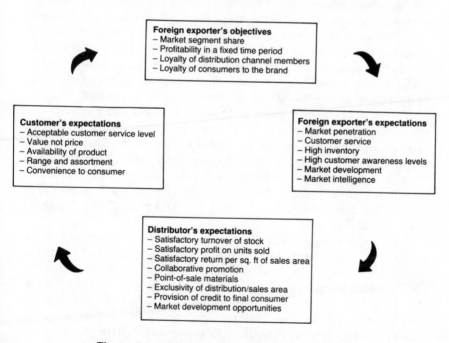

Figure 7.1 Is there any synergy in the system?

research that tells us about the possible reaction to certain brands and therefore the economic feasibility for them to enter the market.

If everyone pulls together the task is easy. A great deal will depend, then, upon market conditions, distribution infrastructure, consumer reaction and the willingness of the exporter in question not just to invest, but to experiment with the necessary resource and be wildly innovative when the occasion requires it.

Trends in place of sale/distribution

Efficiencies are being sought in this area. Worldwide the trend is towards shorter distribution channels and closer links, if not direct relationships, with those active participants in the channel. The length of the distribution channel between producer and consumer worldwide has become steadily shorter, to the point now where many producers, mainly in personal computers, for example, are moving into direct sale. Only in Japan, because of traditional complex cross-company ownership ties, are distribution channels long, but even there this anachronism is being challenged. Instead of trying to enter in the traditional way via the existing distribution channels, some Western companies have been successful in Japan because they have short-circuited the traditional Japanese distribution system and gone direct to the Japanese consumer instead. Going direct is clearly a trend in Western markets and provides the manufacturer with the ability to take back more control of the product and the level of service offered to customers. This comes at a price, however. When a manufacturer seeks to take over the tasks of intermediaries in the distribution channel, it requires investment. It requires supplanting what is already in place with something new. While more desirable, it is accompanied by factors relating to both time and money.

Some would argue that the only way to internationalize is to move closer and closer to full control by means of wholly owned subsidiary. This is quite erroneous. First, we have to consider industry characteristics, the value-added of the business and what the customers actually want. Second, it is often possible to achieve close control through a commission agent or a joint venture. Control should not be equated directly with ownership. There is no linear progression, as some academics would argue, that suggests that companies should move from exporting through joint ventures to wholly owned subsidiaries. That is nonsense, but it is nonsense that keeps getting repeated. Where a foreign market is performing above average it should be deserving of more resources. For example, market development may require construction of new out-of-town superstores adjacent to major highways, or perhaps it is an investment required for a computerized reservations system. Whatever the requirement, it will be a call for cash or support for money to be raised in the foreign market, which boils down to the same thing. In any event, levels of service do need to be maintained not only within a country market, but across all markets in which the company is represented.

Impetus for international alliances

Technological:

- Rapid technological change exceeds capability of one firm.
- Technological skills/expertise are more widely dispersed throughout the world than in the past.
- Shorter product life cycles require rapid technological development.
- Improved information flow worldwide eases alliance formation.

Managerial:

- Leverage expertise of foreign firms in their local markets.
- Tailor products to local needs.
- Growth in acceptance of cooperation.
- Difficult to maintain competitive advantage alone, without a global perspective.

Economic/regulatory:

- Enjoy global economies of scale.
- Open new markets to develop synergies and learning curve benefits.
- Attractive way to utilize excess capacity given slower growth in domestic markets.
- Local content laws and other countertrade measures force firms to conduct business with other firms.

Strategic:

- Gain access to otherwise closed markets.
- Take advantage of synergies due to the emergence of products with a global appeal.
- Share risks of competing in a certain market.
- Retaliate/defend against competitors.

Source: Lisa M. Ellram (1992), 'Patterns in international alliances', *Journal of Business Logistics*, **13** (1), p. 3.

However, where a foreign market is underperforming, questions should be asked of the nature and level of representation in that market. It may well be that a wholly owned subsidiary is inappropriate and that there is a well-established distributor with essential credentials who is able to furnish a very high level of customer service as well as to provide a range and assortment of goods for their customers. Where there is any sign of caution, this will be reflected in the representation in that market and the way in which that market is treated by head office in terms of method of quotation, i.e. cash terms. Willingness to do business in that market is an important factor promoting innovation in distribution systems. Countertrade, already mentioned in Chapter 6, is evidence of this. Yet if there is a willingness to do business alongside a set of country characteristics quite foreign to the home market, this will often lead to a joint venture being established.

Hybrid forms abound and it is wrong to think of foreign direct investment and the wholly owned subsidiary as being the most desirable or ultimate solution. If the desire is to milk the foreign market in the short term, that can be done through exporting, or even 'dumping', a product.

ISO 9000: defining quality amongst carriers

ISO, the International Organization for Standardization, includes the national standards bodies of ninety-one countries. The American National Standards Institute (ANSI) is a member body representing the United States. ISO's objective is to promote development of standardization and related world activities to facilitate international exchange of goods and services and to develop cooperation in intellectual, scientific, technological and economic activity. The results of ISO technical work are published as international standards.

ISO 9000 was created to provide standards in the area of quality management and quality assurance standards with a common language for a global audience. The ISO 9000 Series is a set of five individual but related international standards on quality management and quality assurance. They can be used by manufacturing and service industries alike. These standards were developed to document the quality system elements needed for an efficient quality system in your company.

Corporations around the globe have been building and continue to build their quality systems around these standards. Both large and small companies with international businesses perceive the ISO 9000 Series as a route to open markets and improved competitiveness.

Increasingly, European customers expect US companies to have their quality systems registered to ISO 9001, 9002 or 9003. This generally involves having an accredited independent third party conduct an on-site audit of your company's operations against the requirements of the appropriate standard. Successful completion of this audit means your company will receive a registration certificate identifying your quality system as complying with ISO 9001, 9002 or 9003. Your company also will be listed in a register maintained by the accredited third-party registration organization. You may publicize your registration and use the third-party registrar's certification mark on your advertising, letterheads and other publicity materials, but not on your products.

The United States adopted the ISO 9000 Series as the ANSI/ASQC Q90 Series. If you would like more information on the ANSI/ASQC Q90 Series, contact the American Society for Quality Control.

Source: Helen L. A. Richardson (1991), 'Moving toward global safety', *Transportation and Distribution*, November, p. 30.

Repatriation of capital can be achieved in a number of ways including management fees, loans, royalties, etc. There is no one ideal mode of market entry. In fact, the form that is arousing the most interest internationally is franchising, yet, ironically, for all the reasons that make control desirable, companies such as McDonald's – famous for its franchising activities in the United States – entered the United Kingdom with wholly owned subsidiaries and only comparatively recently offered some limited franchising opportunities. Franchising offers the consumer the same reassurance as that of a brand. Standardization to common norms therefore has to be in place for a franchising operation to be successful. As an international mode of market entry, it is prominent in a range of activities including hotels, restaurants, car rental and fast food and a whole host of services for the office, the home and the individual.

Trade-offs in setting customer service levels

Basically this comes down to costs. Ideally, every marketer would wish to offer a high level of customer service, but this may in fact prove to be unfeasible in terms of costs relative to the contribution received.

Trade-offs start with the choice of distribution coverage to be adopted:

- Extensive distribution (a penetration strategy) seeking the maximum number of sales outlets. A high-volume/low-value distribution strategy.

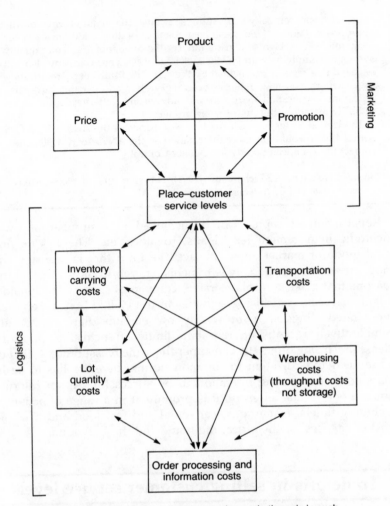

Marketing objective: allocate resources to the marketing mix in such a manner as to maximize the long-run profitability of the firm.
Logistics objective: minimize total costs given the customer service objective.
Where total costs equal transportation costs + warehousing costs + order processing and information costs + lot quantity costs + inventory carrying costs.

Figure 7.2 Cost trade-offs in marketing and logistics. (Source: adapted from Douglas M. Lambert, 1978, *The Development of an Inventory Costing Methodology: A study of the cost associated with holding inventory*, National Council of Physical Distribution Management: Chicago, IL, p. 7, as reported in James R. Stock and Douglas M. Lambert, 1987, *Strategic Logistics Management*, 2nd edn, Richard D. Irwin: Homewood, IL, p. 42. Reprinted with the permission of the publisher.)

- Selective distribution, i.e. selected by the producer.
- Exclusive distribution where the manufacturer is looking for something beyond selective distribution. First, this is a high-value/low-volume distribution strategy. Distribution outlets are targeted in terms of profile of the customer base and the outlet has to reflect the status, prestige and quality of the product not only in terms of the sales side, but also in after-sales care.

Commonly these will be the first questions to be broached. Of course, if the supplier is willing to absorb some of the cost, then this may change the equation slightly, if, for example, help is offered to an otherwise acceptable intermediary to enable them to reach the desired standard. Alternatively, the supplier may choose to go solo.

Customer expectations in terms of level of service are important. Parts and service may be required and this, too, may influence the decision to go with intermediaries. Holding parts may require holding substantial inventory which, in turn, means costs for the intermediary, so turnover rates as well as discounts offered by the supplier would be all important in the agreement. Inventory levels and inventory location are also important decisions and are influenced by the choice of transportation to be used. Air freight can reduce waiting times for parts anywhere in Europe to a matter of hours. The costs, however, have to be recovered from the value-added in the product.

Credit is another expectation of the trade intermediary looking at the supplier, but cashflow is often something that the supplier is seeking from the distribution channel. Franchising, for example, is a good means of distribution, and an excellent means of raising cash for a supplier with a market-proven idea. Franchising pushes risk down the channel and cash upwards. Financial stability is something that a supplier may seek of franchising but, equally, a financially unstable company would not be able to provide any coherent credit policy.

Trade-offs cannot be arbitrary. These are policy decisions taken in the light of distribution channel method and members' needs. There are, however, issues relating to power, coercion and reward. Culturally there may be important differences across nations in this regard. Commonly, we see strategic alliances taking place with regard to the Single European Market. A new form of acceptable corporate behaviour has been forced on companies, of either seeking a partner with which to work or of going to their death alone. Strategic alliances now take place between companies of equal size and often of a similar technological level, either to work on research and development or to share market costs. Between companies there may well have been intense rivalry which has now melted, faced with exigency. Cross-culturally, negotiation is a difficult task because success is so uncertain. Within the same market it may be possible to persuade two companies of similar size to merge their operations into one. Sometimes governments have taken this task of persuasion upon themselves, supposedly acting in the national interest. However, when we start to consider negotiating a strategic alliance between two companies from different countries, cultural factors enter into the reckoning. Whereas in the home market it may be possible for two companies to see advantages in an alliance, i.e. that both are gaining from a partnership, there are other markets in the world where this is plainly not so. Instead of a win/win situation, mistrust of the foreign company may be such that only a win/lose outcome may be acceptable. That is to say that I may find your proposal acceptable only if I can go back to my superiors and show what we are winning from the deal and what you are prepared to sacrifice for our involvement.

Once any such agreement is under way, thoughts then turn to evaluation: in other words, monitoring the foreign operations and considering means of control. At this juncture, you then have to consider how to handle power, how to reward and how to enforce what you want to achieve in the foreign market. Power, coercion and rewards are a very sensitive area of operation. Motivation is usually considered in terms of financial inducement, but what if you have a fairly successful, but not startlingly successful, Middle East agent? They are probably sub-optimizing but earning more than they need, so further financial incentives are useless. Equally, efforts at coercion may be hopelessly misapplied and culturally the worst possible thing to do in the circumstances. There has to be some degree of flexibility, otherwise you have only a problem, not a market.

Checklist: be aware

Beware xenophobia	Curb your own xenophobic instincts which are bound to arise, the more dissimilar the foreign market is to your own domestic market.

Brand equity	The goodwill created by customer loyalty has an important balance sheet effect that has to be recognized.
Trade distribution channel impact on costs	Impact of distribution channel chosen on costs and thus final prices?
Trade distribution channel loyalty	The larger market development is the issue here. Retaining and motivating good channel intermediaries is important.
Channel Tunnel	This has been delayed way beyond the original June 1993 opening date, now passed. However, this will be the first time that the United Kingdom has been joined to the mainland of Europe, physically and psychologically.
Customer acceptance	There may be a gap with 'desires', but how wide or narrow is this gap? How forgiving is this customer of past service? There is a radical difference between 'acceptable' levels in the United Kingdom and North America.
Customer desires	The ultimate that the customer desires. Often a trade-off takes place because of either income or availability.
Database marketing	Computerized segmentation of entire nations by neighbourhood is now possible revealing social, economic and lifestyle data, that can be used by marketers to target groups effectively. The cost of maintaining one name and address is 1 cent in 1993, whereas it was $7.14 in 1984 because the technology was not so easily available. At the same time, a sales call costs between $225 and $275.
Determine level of service	Determine the required level of service to be provided which will in turn impact on physical distribution flows, warehousing, transportation and inventory levels.
Diffusion of innovation	Depends upon the society, its materialism, levels of disposable income and how people respond culturally to change.
Direct mail	Commonly referred to as 'junk mail', it uses computer databases to target goods and services at individuals. While sometimes annoying to the individual, as an industry it is effective.
Economic environmental uncertainty	No one is going to commit long-term resources to an unstable environment. Political and economic uncertainty may be present.
Ethnic marketing	Ethnic marketing is another form of segmentation. In the United States there is a part-time Muslim cable television channel, as well as a Nashville country and

western channel. These present focused opportunities, provided that the correct approach is made in addressing these groups.

Experience, credibility and performance of the foreign intermediary

These require investigation in the first instance and constant monitoring thereafter. Customer surveys may provide some important information for action. Compare actual information with anticipated performance and take any corrective action.

Export overhead administration

Check the overhead administrative expense being charged to export sales. Is it reasonable or will it prevent export sales from ever being profitable?

Financial needs

Distribution channel members seek investment not just in their means of servicing clients but perhaps also in offering credit to the final consumer.

Freight choice issues

Time, transhipment, cost, potential spoilage, inventory and warehousing are all factors to be considered. Note that couriers such as TNT or UPS are now pan-European, ahead of proposed changes taking place.

Intermediary expectations

Collaboration on promotion as well as offering consumer credit. If successful, market expansion and market development opportunities.

International sourcing

Final goods for sale are sold by their brand name, not the country of origin. Where on occasion it is home-produced, this is worth emphasizing. Elsewhere, beware of tariffs on product entry.

Knowing the customer

Action taken must at all times make sense when considering the final goal – the customer.

Pan-European distribution systems

These can be expected following the opening of the Channel Tunnel. The French have already invested heavily.

Pre-inspection services

Where goods have to be inspected prior to shipment. Failure to do this will mean only that the goods are auctioned at the port of arrival.

Product learning

How do people learn and from whom? Who are the opinion leaders and change agents in this society?

Product life cycle

Products mature and, as they change, you have to reduce costs in your distribution also. Be prepared to move with the market and anticipate changes in distribution necessary for your product before they become apparent.

Ratio of old to new clients

Analyze ratios of new to old clients to determine turnover.

Ratio of value-added in export sales

Analyze ratios of value-added to volume of total foreign sales.

Store audits	Check for availability of A. C. Neilsen in-store audits* for packaged goods.
Strategic alliance patterns	What drives an alliance is complex. It may be chiefly to do with resources, but this includes research and development, marketing and market sharing.
Sub-cultural distribution needs	Within a youth market there are often several sub-cultures; for example, over the years we have had 'hippies' and 'punks' each of which conformed to a certain dress style.
Substitutability	Products may be bought in a number of different forms of outlets ranging from specialist and department stores to direct sale or even vending machines.
Total export costs	Ensure that profitability is reflected against total expenditure outlay assessed on that market.
Trade associations	Check out trade associations wherever they exist e.g. Chemical Industry.
Training	Train distributor's and agent's sales staff.
Warranty	Ensure that adequate warranty coverage is being provided, including parts, service and maintenance. This includes resources in both people skills and investment in equipment.

*System of continuous research whereby a panel of recruited retailers has invoices and stocks audited periodically so that shares of market held by different brands can be determined by their movement from shops. A. C. Neilsen Co. Ltd specialize in shop audits.

References and further reading

Allen, Kathleen M. (1991), 'The role of logistics in the overseas plant selection decision process of United States-based multinational corporations', *Journal of Business Logistics*, **12** (2), pp. 59–72

Butler, Jack (1988), *The Importer's Handbook*, Woodhead-Faulkner: Cambridge

Byrne, Patrick (1992), 'Logistics in Europe: Success will require radical changes', *Transportation and Distribution*, October, pp. 60–3

Cannon, Tom and Mike Willis (1986), *How to Buy and Sell Overseas*, Hutchinson: London

Daily Telegraph (1988), *How to Export*, Daily Telegraph Business Enterprise Books: London

Ellram, Lisa M. (1992), 'Patterns in international alliances', *Journal of Business Logistics*, **13** (1), pp. 1–25

Helper, Donald G. and H. Chang Moon (1990), 'Striving for first-rate markets in Third World nations', *Management Review*, May, pp. 20–2

Klein, Saul and Victor J. Roth (1993), 'Satisfaction with international marketing channels', *Journal of the Academy of Marketing Science*, **21** (1), pp. 39–44

Moore, Richard A. (1991), 'Relationship states in an international marketing channel', *European Journal of Marketing*, **25** (5), pp. 47–59

Morris, Mag (1985), *Importing for the Small Business*, Kogan Page: London

Murphy, Paul R., Douglas R. Dalenberg and James M. Daley (1991), 'Analysing international water transportation: The perspectives of large U.S. industrial corporations', *Journal of Business Logistics*, **12** (1), pp. 169–90

Murphy, Paul R., James M. Daley and Douglas R. Dalenberg (1991a), 'Forwarders are a vital link for shippers', *Transportation and Distribution*, August, p. 44

Murphy, Paul R., James M. Daley and Douglas R. Dalenberg (1991b), 'Smaller shippers play important global role', *Transportation and Distribution*, December, pp. 41–9

Richardson, Helen L. A. (1991), 'Moving toward global safety', *Transportation and Distribution*, November, pp. 29–33

Semple, Jack (1992), 'A pan-Europe problem', *Management Today*, June, pp. 101–2

Stock, James R. and Douglas M. Lambert (1987), *Strategic Logistics Management*, 2nd edn, Richard D. Irwin: Homewood, IL, p. 42

Trunick, Perry A. (1992a), 'British transportation goes commercial', *Transportation and Distribution*, April, pp. 49–54

Trunick, Perry A. (1992b), 'Europe: A single market with complex logistics', *Transportation and Distribution*, October, pp. 51–63

Welch, Mary (1993), 'Database marketing explodes', *Business Marketing*, March, pp. 48–80

Wortzel, Lawrence H. and Heidi Vernon Wortzel (1981), 'Export marketing strategies for NIC and LDC-based firms', *Columbia Journal of World Business*, Spring, pp. 51–60

8

Planning and control

'Planning and control' is the management dictum of yesterday. Today the dictum is 'employee empowerment' and the management of change. Yet to some headquarters back at home in another country, it may be seen to be very necessary to have some form of planning and control. Ideally this also has to allow the foreign subsidiary some form of flexibility in operations so that it can operate in a loose/tight atmosphere as recommended by Peters and Waterman's *In Search of Excellence* (1982).

Focusing on global strategy, Yip (1989) looked at what he called industry globalization 'drivers': market, cost, government and competitive market conditions. These drivers depend on customer behaviour and the structure of distribution channels, and if we could recognize these we may then perhaps be able to decide when best to employ global strategy levers. Yip states quite clearly that more than one type of international strategy can be viable in a given industry (see Table 8.1).

However, it has to be remembered that, as we talk of world trade, we are dealing effectively only with trade between developed nations. Africa and South America are two areas comprising 20 per cent of the world's population, but their share of world trade is minuscule. In 1990 South America had 4 per cent, whereas Africa, which had 4.8 per cent in 1980, had only 2.2 per cent in 1988. To some degree this reflects developing-country exposure to exports focused on commodities. While the developed countries have preferential treatment in place for their exports, the world price of commodities is generally low but is also capable of being volatile.

Table 8.1 Effects of industry globalization drivers on the potential use of global strategy levers.

Industry drivers	Strategy levers				
	Major market participation	Product standardization	Activity concentration	Uniform marketing	Integrated competitive moves
Market					
Homogeneous needs	Fewer varieties needed to serve many markets	Standardized product is more acceptable			Allows sequenced invasion of markets
Global customers			Marketing process has to be coordinated	Marketing content needs to be uniform	
Global channels			Marketing process has to be coordinated	Marketing content needs to be uniform	
Transferable marketing	Easier to expand internationally			Allows use of global brands/advertising, etc.	
Cost					
Economies of scale and scope	Multiple markets needed to reach economic scale	Standardization needed to reach economic scale	Concentration helps reach economic scale	Uniform marketing cuts programme development and production costs	Country interdependence affects overall scale economies
Learning and experience	Multiple markets accelerate learning	Standardization accelerates learning	Concentration accelerates learning		
Sourcing efficiencies			Centralized purchasing exploits efficiencies		
Favourable logistics	Easier to expand internationally		Allows concentrated production		Allows export competition

	Market participation	Product standardization	Activity concentration	Uniform marketing	Competitive moves
Differences in country costs and skills					Increase vulnerability of high-cost countries
Product development costs	Multiple markets needed to pay back investment	Standardization reduces development needs	Exploited by activity concentration / Concentration cuts cost of development		
Government					
Favourable trade policies	Affects nature/extent of participation	May require or prevent product features	Local content rules affect extent of concentration possible		Integration needed to deal with competitive effects of tariffs/subsidies
Compatible technical standards	Affects markets that can be entered	Affects standardization possible			
Common marketing regulations				Affects approaches possible	
Competitive					
Interdependence of countries	More participation leverages benefits	Accept trade-offs to get best global product	Locate key activities in lead countries	Use lead country to develop programmes	Integration needed to exploit benefits
Competitors globalized or might globalize	Expand to match or pre-empt	Match or pre-empt	Match or pre-empt	Match or pre-empt	Integration needed to exploit benefits

Source: George S. Yip (1989), 'Global strategy: In a world of nations?', *Sloan Management Review*, **31**, Fall, pp. 29–41.

Sheth (1977) argued that the ultimate opportunity lay outside the United States, a view that was then seen to be almost heretical and pointed to several important limitations:

1. No systematic and continuous assessment of buyer needs and expectations, most marketing research being post factum, to find out whether a new concept or product developed by R & D will be acceptable to customers.

2. Marketing research is on a country-by-country basis whereas potential markets are mostly in the metropolitan areas, especially in the less developed countries. Clustering metropolitan areas both within and between countries is more meaningful from a marketing viewpoint. Moreover, we still find greater similarity between metropolitan areas across countries than within countries.

3. Assessment of customer needs and expectations should be based on data collected at the micro level, namely the household or business unit.

Sheth's analysis is on customer needs, not the product. Buyer expectations are determined by the social environment in which consumers become conditioned to establishing choice criteria in specific buying situations as a result of family, reference groups, lifestyle, social stratification and culture, including ethnic subcultures. Marketing programmes are likely to be differentiated from one segment of the world market to another. The model encourages the multinational corporation to look at the world as a potential marketplace. It emphasizes greater customer-oriented marketing planning, and points to the need to go beyond secondary data. Finally, it seeks to place marketing research in the context of the multinational (see Figure 8.1).

Foreign markets can be planned and controlled

We are well past the stage where a product could be identified as being solely of one national origin. To compete with foreign firms, domestic firms will often source various inputs so as to either lower their overall costs or assure themselves of supply, or will perhaps

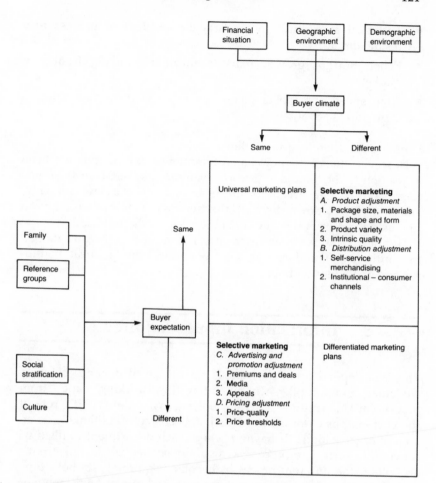

Figure 8.1 A scheme for differentiated marketing programmes. (Source: Jagdish N. Sheth, 1977, 'A market-oriented strategy of long-range planning for multinational corporations', *European Research*, January, pp. 3–12.)

enter into a research, development and design partnership with the foreign supplier for an entire product line. Global sourcing can provide the following, according to Fagan (1991):

• Available demand.
• Uniqueness of global supply for the particular product.
• Quality assurance together with product availability and lower costs.

- Technical supremacy for a particular product or process may reside abroad.
- Penetration of growth markets through sourcing from that market.
- High speed of supplier response can be vital in maintaining a competitive advantage.

Sourcing can then lead to market entry.

However, one of the key changes in managerial thinking has been in relation to the 'boundaryless' company, or as the GE 1990 Annual Report put it: 'Our dream for the 1990s is a boundaryless company, where we knock down the walls that separate us from each other on the inside and from our key constituencies on the outside.'

The new boundaries are more psychological than organizational: the 'authority' boundary, the 'task' boundary, the 'political' boundary and the 'identity' boundary.

Information inputs required

This will depend upon the actual and perceived distance between customer and supplier. In an interesting working paper from Stockholm University in Sweden, Solveig Wikstrom (1993) wrote of the customer as co-producer. This has been seen traditionally as an area of organizational behaviour where each department fulfilled its function in turn. The process was simply sequential. In Wikstrom's argument, the different processes become compressed in both time and place; the value-creating process is shifted forward and now lies in the requirements, demands and problems of the customer.

The company is in charge of its destiny; it is driving, not being driven. It can involve external parties so as to tailor its market offering and market performance better. It can collaborate with competitors so as to improve the value-added to customers. Wikstrom sees technology as having enabled companies to function as they could not do before, and this leads to a redistribution of roles for, once companies are able, for example, to produce their own graphics through desktop publishing, it diminishes the role of the advertising agency. Each action produces a reaction – a basic law of physics. However, Wikstrom sees this customer co-production operating at three different levels:

1. Where the customer composes the input on the basis of various modules offered by the supplier.

2. Where the customer draws up specifications, often in collaboration with the supplier. This is a stage at which a great deal of interaction takes place. In personal care, e.g. dentistry, a standardized care product is modified according to the individual's special requirements and demands. In the business-to-business sphere, almost all work is subcontracted according to specification.

3. Pure co-production means customer and supplier collaborating throughout the whole value-creating process. Systems solutions are a good example from bank services, accounting systems and traffic surveillance systems. It is happening in the consumer market also, in that professionals, including healthcare professionals, now actually consider the views of the patients.

Recent reports on the US economy have challenged the myth that US manufacturing is in decline. Productivity per person had increased, but employment was down. 'Downsizing' or 'rightsizing' has taken place in all branches of manufacturing and pay has held steady. Manufacturers' exports are on the increase, and Honda alone has exported 100,000 cars from the United States. However, this has taken place in all Western markets. Nevertheless, there is yet another interesting measure of the productivity of intellectual output in terms of patent registrations. In 1990, the United States

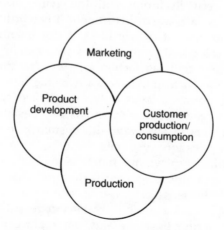

Figure 8.2 Information drives the cycle.

registered 30.1 per cent of international patent registrations, as opposed to 24.2 per cent for Japan and 16.5 per cent for Germany. In 1987, the United States had 25.16 per cent and the Japanese 25.88 per cent. This will take time to show through in terms of economic figures, but the research investment is clearly there and should become visible in future years. However, a *Fortune* article of 21 September 1992 ranks flexibility high in Japan's manufacturing strategy, but not in America's. It is possible then that you, individually, are doing well, but relative to what? The nature of competition is that it is intense. It requires more than just a single stride – it means forever moving forward to provide the best for the least.

Too many firms, including the giant American car firms, are too interested in their own reflection to try to consider what the market actually wants. Consider their overriding concern with selling on price and, consequently, cost reduction. Compare advertising for their products with that of Japanese competitors. Simple insertion of added features at a low price does not create added value for the customer, who is only too aware that the American variant may not work as well, or at all, relative to its foreign competitor, even if domestically built.

Car manufacturers use customer questionnaires that give them the answers they want to hear, e.g. when you received the car, was it clean? The question does not ask or invite responses about possible complaints that could or should be remedied. The car could have been collected and found to have literally dozens of faults, but the questionnaire concerns itself only with the civility of the sales force and car cleaning. As a research instrument it is worthless, and as a public relations exercise it is worthless if not insulting. The real intent is to find sales leads through this snowballing technique of asking about your overall satisfaction and whether anyone in your family is likely to want to purchase a car in the immediate future. This form of questionnaire looks only for satisfied customers who can provide sales leads, it cannot and is not designed to correct product faults or deal in any way with customer complaints. This information is for sales force use only.

Mystery shopping surveys are much more likely to reveal true consumer beliefs and attitudes towards products. Assessors, as they are called, have to be selected as appropriate for the age range that they are investigating, but such surveys can reveal a consumer's true perspective of the business and can highlight unacceptable waiting times for service and whether sales staff require product training or simply need to be informed about civility when dealing with the buying public. Complaints can be useful in targeting company weaknesses and monitoring standards of goods and services, and therefore in raising overall quality. This increases the chances of 'getting it right first time' and also of solving individual problems. It pays to address dissatisfaction because, for one thing, a very high proportion of customers will not complain, but simply vote with their feet and take their business elsewhere. Approximately twice as many dissatisfied customers as satisfied customers will tell others of their experiences. Generally a dissatisfied customer will tell at least eight other people. Besides, it is seven times harder to gain a new customer than it is to regain an old one. On the basis of profitability existing customers, particularly those who have been with you a year or two, are more profitable because you now have the information on their needs: you have their profile.

Principles of total quality management

General:

1. Get to know the next and final customer.
2. Get to know the direct competition and the world-class leaders (whether competitors or not).
3. Dedicate to continual, rapid improvement in quality, response time, flexibility and cost.
4. Achieve unified purpose via extensive sharing of information and involvement in planning and implementation of change.

Design and organization:

5. Cut the number of components or operations and number of suppliers to a few good ones.
6. Organize resources into chains of customers, each chain mostly self-contained and focused on a product or customer 'family'.

Operations:

7. Cut flow time, distance, inventory and space along the chain of customers.
8. Cut set-up, change-over, get-ready and start-up time.
9. Operate at the customer's rate of use (or a smoothed representation of it).

Human resource development:

10. Continually invest in human resources through cross-training (for mastery), education, job switching and multi-year cross-career reassignments; and improved health, safety and security.

---

11. Develop operator-*owners* of products, processes and outcomes via broadened owner-like reward and recognition.

Quality and process improvement:

12. Make it easier to produce or provide the product without mishap or process variation.
13. Record and *own* quality, process and mishap data at the workplace.
14. Ensure that front-line associates get first chance at process improvement – before staff experts.

Accounting and control:

15. Cut transactions and reporting; control *causes* and measure performance at the source, not via periodic cost reports.

Capacity:

16. Maintain/improve present resources and human work before thinking about new equipment and automation.
17. Automate incrementally when process variability cannot otherwise be reduced.
18. Seek to have multiple work stations, machines, flow lines, cells for each product or customer family.

Marketing and sales:

19. Market and sell your firm's increasing customer-oriented capabilities and competencies.

Source: Richard J. Schonberger (1992), 'Is strategy strategic? Impact of total quality management on strategy', *Academy of Management Executive*, 6 (3), pp. 80–7. Reprinted by permission of publisher, from *Management Review*, May 1990 © 1990. American Management Association, New York. All rights reserved.

A survey undertaken by the Association for Manufacturing Excellence (Moody, 1992) set out to determine what characteristics suppliers use to describe a 'best customer'. From a list of twenty-four possible characteristics, respondents from procurement, sales and sub-contract administration rated the following as the most importar.c:

- Early supplier involvement.
- Mutual trust.
- Involvement in product design.
- Quality initiatives.
- Profitability.
- Schedule sharing.

- Response to cost reduction ideas.
- Communication and feedback.
- Crisis management/response.
- Commitment to partnership.

Characteristics that were not rated very high were negotiation and award process, schedule stability, technology sharing, and training and education.

Competitive leverage analysis is a form of quadrant analysis that uses consumers' stated discriminating features to differentiate between competing products such as safety or even industry accreditation. It is based on respondent information captured in several market research survey questions: first, a series of questions concerning product use and preference; second, a question that rates or ranks importance of selected features of a product or service; and third, a question that rates the performance of the major competitors on each feature. The discriminating power is derived from the performance ratings of each competitor on every feature. A conventional discriminant analysis may be run. From the results, a scale is developed based on the percentage of explained performance variance. This scale takes into account the contribution that each feature makes to each discriminant function and the contribution that each discriminant function makes to the total productive power of the analysis.

The x and y axes reflect importance and discriminating power (see Figure 8.3). The farther to the right that the feature is located, the more important it is to respondents. The higher that the feature is positioned, the higher its discriminating value. Each feature is depicted by a bubble, and the size and pattern, whether filled or empty, indicate how the feature is perceived within the industry as a whole. An empty bubble denotes below-average performance and its size denotes the distance from average performance.

Quadrant 1: Entry tickets or unmet needs. Features in the lower right quadrant, while highly important, lack power to discriminate. Entry tickets are where the industry as a whole is performing well. However, empty bubbles will reflect unmet needs.

Quadrant 2: Hot buttons. Features in the upper right quadrant are critical, considered highly important and highly discriminatory. Most often discovered in new, emerging,

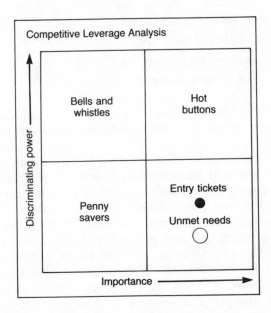

Figure 8.3 Competitive leverage analysis. (Source: Joel C. Webster, 1991, 'Technique surpasses standard quadrant analysis', *Marketing News*, 2 September, pp. 8–9.)

vulnerable markets. Firms should act quickly to adopt them.

Quadrant 3: Bells and whistles. Upper left quadrant consists of features considered less important yet highly discriminating. If the cost of improving performance on one or more of these features is relatively low, it is usually advantageous for a company to invest in products in this quadrant. Bells and whistles help to differentiate a product and increase its appeal to customers.

Quadrant 4: Penny savers. Contains features neither important nor discriminating. Improvements will produce only minor results in performance. Hold off on investment in this area.

Competitive Leverage Analysis can be used regularly over time to track brands and make changes in market response.

Assessing and evaluating foreign market information

Europe is currently undergoing profound change as a result of alliances leading to an ever more dominant European Community and its role in world trade. Perhaps as a counterbalance to this, there has been the North American Free Trade Agreement (NAFTA), but this is significantly different in origin and intention. NAFTA is about free trade, whereas the European Community is about a customs union leading to ever-increasing harmonization measures so as to effectively dismantle national frontiers. NAFTA, by way of comparison, is far removed from that ideal. Whereas Europe has a few key players following Germany, including France and the United Kingdom, NAFTA is dominated by the United States, and the only reason that Mexico and Canada are involved is the dominant power of their neighbour. Mexico stands to usurp Canada's position as supplier to the United States, and Canada realizes that if it does nothing, then it will lose totally. The presence of NAFTA does not mean that free trade presently takes place either between those countries or within them. Canada has a number of protected industries, including brewing, that do not practise free trade within Canada. Clearly the impetus for change has come from outside.

As change takes place, information becomes important – information on the nature, magnitude and implications of that change or series of changes and how this will affect corporate strategy, for example:

- Dismantling of trade frontiers to EC member states.
- Marketization practices in the former Eastern Europe now implementing privatization schemes.
- Creation of free mobility of labour, trade and investment within the EC.
- Appearance of pan-European mergers and alliances to compete in this new EC environment.
- Doubts about the degree to which there is a homogeneous market across the Common Market (there isn't!).
- Development of institutions arising directly from these changes either to research, disseminate and teach pan-European issues or

else to provide a new unified European competitor in key strategic areas including telecommunications.

Cerruti and Holtzman (1990) identified four different strategies with regard to the new Europe:

1. Global mega-players who happen to be active also in Europe, but who have global functional skills and global financial clout.

2. Geographic niche players who are particularly good at targeting personalized or localized needs and appeal. Mostly small to medium-sized firms with limited geographical scope and tightly integrated supply and distribution chains.

3. Pan-European specialists with a national or regional presence in several European markets in closely related product/service areas. Carrefour is a primarily geographic niche-player in France, now moving aggressively towards a pan-European position in hypermarket retailing.

4. Portfolio players include multi-industry diversified firms such as Hanson Trust. These companies are not committed to long-term positions in any given industry, but rather make their acquisitions for their asset appreciation potential. Points of leverage for such competitors are superior corporate finance skills and perhaps turnaround expertise.

These strategies are not mutually exclusive and are depicted in Figure 8.4.

At the micro level, companies have to judge who their competitors are. Who is it exactly that they are competing with, against what products or services and on what terms? This may sound very familiar to anyone who read Theodore Levitt's seminal article in the *Harvard Business Review* in the 1960s on 'Marketing Myopia'. Robert (1990) takes this a stage further and suggests how market knowledge of your competitors can turn them into followers:

• Determine which competitors your strategy will attract.

• Anticipate each potential competitor's future strategy.

• Draw competitive profiles where each competitor will put its emphasis and de-emphasis in terms of products, users and geographic markets.

• Manage the competitor's strategy. A 'copycat' strategy can lure a competitor into a foreign market and bid on a deal, only to beat off the competition. This may, however, have been the express

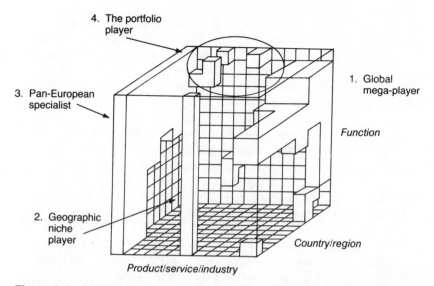

Figure 8.4 Four generic strategies are emerging in Europe. (Source: James L. Cerruti and Joseph Holtzman, 1990, 'Business strategy in the new European landscape', *Journal of Business Strategy*, November–December, p. 22. © 1990, *Journal of Business Strategy*, Faulkner and Gray Publishers, New York, NY. Reprinted with permission.)

intent. It is a 'poison pill' strategy to kill off competitors who get too close to you.

- Neutralize the competitor's areas of excellence, whether in customer service, distribution or industry knowledge.

- Choose your competitors, do not let your competitors choose you. No company has the resources to compete with all competitors, nor does it need to do so.

These strategic elements focus, however, more on competitors than customers and so are more similar to military warfare strategies than marketing strategies, unless it is decided that a customer's focus will be the corporate mission around which all strategy will be devised – then the concept of meeting and exceeding the market leader's customer service levels begins to make sense. Segmentation has become a potent worldwide marketing tool and strategic alliances are becoming an increasingly common means of exploring such market potential.

Coca-Cola is a company large enough in resources to be able to play world markets with ease. It identifies its product market as being in the age range of 12–24 years and although much of its worldwide business could be seen to be concentrated in Mexico, Brazil, Japan and Germany, a 1988 interview with Ira C. Herbert, the Chief Marketing Officer, showed some insights as to how Coca-Cola assesses and perceives market potential in the 155 countries in which it is represented:

> Coke executives can only imagine the possibilities that exist in Indonesia, where 180 million people drink only 3.2 servings of Coke products a year (per capita consumption in the United States, or the number of eight-ounce servings for every man, woman, and child last year, was 274: in Japan, it was 89; in Great Britain, 63). Compare this with China, where annual consumption was just two tenths of a serving for each of its 1.1 billion people. The company's biggest tasks are to make its products more available and to convince consumers that they should drink soft drinks instead of (or in addition to) other beverages.

Herbert therefore goes on to recommend an overall strategy of 'think globally, but act locally'.

A longer-term horizon for investment

Time bears costs. Processes whereby decisions and therefore investments are made have to take place in an ever-shorter time frame because of increased competition and shortening product life cycles which threaten products with obsolescence just months after first launch. As Wikstrom put it: the customer offerings which can be produced most quickly will also contain the latest and most advanced knowledge and will thus also possess the highest value charge. Dogged determination to stick with tradition creates a victory for shortsightedness and undermines the creation of value. Intelligence can be pushed to one side, however, when the fear of the unknown is great and superstitious business practices then hold sway, i.e. going into the market once everyone else is in there, losing out on the 'prime mover' advantage and sometimes the market itself.

Interestingly, Hamel and Prahalad (1989) state their belief that the application of concepts such as strategic fit (between resources and opportunities), 'generic strategies' (low cost vs. differential vs. focus) and the 'strategy hierarchy' (goals, strategies and tactics) have often abetted the process of competitive decline. Competitor analysis focuses on the existing resources (human, technical and financial) of present competitors. The only companies seen as a threat are those with the resources to erode margins and market share in the next planning period. This leaves out those companies with medium- or longer-term ambitions to own the market, and Hamel and Prahalad term this obsession 'strategic intent'. Against this, planners are projecting the present forward incrementally. Hamel and Prahalad go on to say that, whereas the traditional view of strategy focuses on the degree of fit between existing resources and current opportunities, strategic intent creates an extreme misfit between resources and ambitions. Responding to this challenge requires top management to act as follows:

- Create a sense of urgency.

- Develop a competitor focus at every level through widespread rise of competitive intelligence.

- Provide employees with the skills they need to work effectively.

- Give the organization time to digest one challenge before launching another.

- Establish clear milestones and review mechanisms.

Strategic intent means fundamentally changing the game in ways that disadvantage incumbents. Hamel and Prahalad point to the Japanese using four strategies: building layers of advantage, searching for loose bricks, changing the terms of engagement and competing through collaboration. Hamel and Prahalad attack the elitism of strategy formulation and the annual planning ritual whereby the starting point for next year's strategy will almost always be this year's strategy and so improvements are incremental. The company sticks to the segments and territories it knows, whereas the opportunities may be elsewhere. Instead it requires the involvement of everyone in the revitalization, in motivation and in developing faith in the organization's own ability to deliver stated goals.

Checklist: be aware

Ambiguity	There is no place for this. With important documents, ask someone else to check for ambiguity.
Buyer needs and expectations	Focus on the gap between the two. It could be quite revealing and open up a competitive (dis)advantage.
Competitive leverage analysis	Quadrant analysis assessing how consumers discriminate between competitive offerings and the weightings they attach to individual features.
Complaint research	Useful means of investigating weaknesses in the competitive offering.
Customer co-production	Working closely with your customer goes beyond ever having a relationship! It means re-orienting your company and the people in it.
Customer value-added	The enhanced product or service valued by customers which helps to differentiate the company from its competitors.
Customer value creation	Lower costs, better quality, better fit, greater speed, greater convenience, better service, extended warranty.
Developing countries	Constitute only a tiny percentage of world trade yet may present interesting opportunities for your company.
EC	Customs union moving closer to economic and political union (which NAFTA will never do). Membership increasing steadily.
Employee empowerment	Delegation of authority to those at the customer interface to enable them to be problem-solvers.
Flexibility	Cannot formally be included in the planning system, but must be present, otherwise an over-formalized head office approach will lead only to confrontation.
Global strategy benefits	Supposedly cost reductions, improved quality of products and programmes; enhanced customer preference and increased competitive leverage.
Head office guidelines	Should be generally and easily available, understandable and capable of implementation.
Marketing research	Focus on segments, not on nations. Focus on customer needs, not products.
Mystery shopping surveys	Employ 'assessors' who have to be in keeping with the product and age range under investigation.
NAFTA	A free trade area of the United States, Canada and Mexico, dominated by the United States.

Pan-Europeanism	The increasing size of the EC and its virtual coming of age as a world player are spawning a number of specialist reports, institutions, surveys, etc.
Strategic focus	Focus should be on strategic issues, not operational problems.
Strategic intent	See Hamel and Prahalad (1989) who emphasize the need to maintain a longer-term view, motivate the workforce and involve them in strategic planning activities.
Strategic planning	Seen often as an incremental change based on last year's plan. Fails to identify market threats.
Value reduction	Where the sum of all the parts is less than the individual components, you have built a Trabant!

References and further reading

Adamson, Colin (1993), 'Evolving complaint procedures', *Managing Service Quality*, **3** (2), pp. 439–44

Belli, Pedro (1991), 'Globalising the rest of the world', *Harvard Business Review*, July–August, pp. 50–5

Carruthers, John C. (1984), 'Technology-driven and market-driven life cycles: Implications for multinational corporate strategy', *Columbia Journal of World Business*, Summer, pp. 56–60

Cerruti, James L. and Joseph Holtzman (1990), 'Business strategy in the new European landscape', *Journal of Business Strategy*, November–December, p. 22

Crainer, Stuart (1990), 'Putting strategy to work', *Marketing Business*, December, pp. 20–1

Douglas, Susan P. and C. Samuel Craig (1989), 'Evolution of global marketing strategy: Scale, scope and synergy', *Columbia Journal of World Business*, Fall, pp. 47–59

Doz, Y. L. and C. K. Prahalad (1991), 'Managing DMNC's: A search for a new paradigm', *Strategic Management Journal*, **12**, pp. 145–64

Fagan, Mark L. (1991), 'A guide to global sourcing', *Journal of Business Strategy*, March–April, pp. 21–5

Flint, Jerry (1993), 'The myth of U.S. manufacturing's decline', *Forbes*, 18 January, pp. 40–2

Godiwalla, Yezdi H. (1986), 'Multinational planning: Developing a global approach', *Long Range Planning*, **19** (2), pp. 110–16

Hamel, Gary and C. K. Prahalad (1985), 'Do you really have a global strategy?', *Harvard Business Review*, July–August, pp. 139–48

Hamel, Gary and C. K. Prahalad (1989), 'Strategic intent', *Harvard Business Review*, May–June, pp. 63–76

Herbert, Ira C. (1988), 'How Coke markets to the world', *Journal of Business Strategy*, September–October, pp. 4–7

Hirschhorn, Larry and Thomas Gilmore (1992), 'The new boundaries of the "boundaryless" corporation', *Harvard Business Review*, May–June, pp. 104–15

Hurst, Stephen (1993), 'Revealed at source', *Managing Service Quality*, 3 (2), pp. 449–52

Jones, Robert E., L. W. Jacobs and W. Van't Spijker (1992), 'Strategic decision processes in international firms', *Management International Review*, 32 (3), pp. 219–36

Levitt, Theodore (1960), 'Marketing myopia', *Harvard Business Review*, July–August, pp. 45–56

Levy, Matthew D. and Soji Teramura (1993), 'Foreign ownership: Study offers Japanese on new agenda', *Management Review*, January, pp. 49–54

Moody, Patricia E. (1992), 'Customer supplier integration: Why being an excellent customer counts', *Business Horizons*, July–August, pp. 52–7

Morais, Richard C. (1993), 'Patently absurd', *Forbes*, 18 January, p. 46

Peters, Thomas J. and Robert H. Waterman (1982), *In Search of Excellence: Lessons from America's best-run companies*, Fitzhenry and Whiteside: New York

Rafferty, James (1987), 'Exit barriers and strategic position in declining markets', *Long Range Planning*, 20 (2), pp. 86–91

Ramanujam, V. and N. Venkatraman (1988), 'Excellence, planning and performance', *Interfaces*, May–June, pp. 23–31

Robert, Michel H. (1990), 'Managing your company's strategy', *Journal of Business Strategy*, March–April, pp. 24–8

Rozon, Bernie (1991), 'Managing a worldwide logistics network', *Materials Management and Distribution*, July, pp. 15–18

Schonberger, Richard J. (1992), 'Is strategy strategic? Impact of total quality management on strategy', *Academy of Management Executive*, 6 (3), pp. 80–7

Sheth, Jagdish N. (1977), 'A market-oriented strategy of long-range planning for multinational corporations', *European Research*, January, pp. 3–12

Starr, Martin K. (1984), 'Global production and operations strategy', *Columbia Journal of World Business*, Winter, pp. 17–22

Stewart, Thomas A. (1992), 'Brace for Japan's hot new strategy', *Fortune*, 126 (6), pp. 62–74

Taylor, William (1991), 'The logic of global business: An interview with ABB's Percy Barnevik', *Harvard Business Review*, March–April, pp. 91–105

Webster, Joel C. (1991), 'Technique surpasses standard quadrant analysis', *Marketing News*, 2 September, pp. 8–9

Wikstrom, Solveig (1993), 'The customer as co-producer', *Studies in Action and Enterprise*, Department of Business Administration, Stockholm University, p. 1993:1

Yavas, Ugur, B. J. Verhage and R. T. Green (1992), 'Global consumer segmentation versus local market orientation: Empirical findings', *Management International Review*, **32** (3), pp. 265–72

Yip, George S. (1989), 'Global strategy: In a world of nations?', *Sloan Management Review*, **31**, Fall, pp. 29–41

9

Precedents

According to the *Oxford English Dictionary*, a precedent is a legal case or decision taken as a guide for subsequent cases or as a justification. A precedent is therefore seen as a decision that is likely to influence all similar cases in the future. It sets a new landmark for what is allowable. In so doing, it sets new levels of expectation. The other aspect of the word 'precedent' is the issue of justification. Precedents influence behaviour and so it is important to understand the significance that they may have in the international marketing context.

Political

All power derives from the top. While trade is not conducted by nations but by companies, the nation-state is still influential; friendly political relations are good for international trade. It is said that politics creates strange bedfellows, but it also creates profitable trading relationships. Trade missions follow in the wake of political visits to capitalize on the goodwill created which, it is hoped, will transfer and become attached not only to all companies from that particular country, but to their products and services as well. As well as trade missions there are international fairs where there is often a national pavilion serviced by staff from the commercial section of the embassy. 'Flying the flag' can be politically expedient, as can trading with certain countries and not others. For this reason a foreign base of operations can best be selected in terms of its appropriateness for servicing its natural or adjoining markets and politically close allies. Politics is everything. Political situations can therefore be assessed so as to select the optimal base for a regional centre of operations. The rationale behind an initial investment in a foreign country may be defensive, as it could be an attempt to realize potential, if not now, at least in the foreseeable future. Much of what drives trade is connected with politics, such as the definition of friendly countries – those countries with which trade treaties are exchanged, thus minimizing tariffs in bilateral trade exchanges. Other very important factors include trade restrictions, the use of export and import licences and the granting of government-backed trade credits. Precedents are continually being set with regard to how much an export credit line is actually worth and over what period, the restrictions of use and the period of time over which it will be operational. Apart from normal trade, politics creates opportunities for countertrade agreements and so for product-related payments and buyer-favourable payment terms or guaranteed sources of supply for a given period of time. Politics brings trading partners together or drives them apart. Its significance cannot be ignored. Yet while the North American Free Trade Agreement is designed to develop free trade within the North American subcontinent, free trade is still to take place within these markets themselves. In Canada, for instance, there are 500 non-tariff trade barriers. Non-tariff trade barriers are the chief problem confronting free trade worldwide. In Canada non-tariff barriers are institutionalized by provincial governments. These have been summarized in terms of the remaining provincial bastions: restrictions on interprovincial commerce including trucking; partisan provincial subsidies; provincial taxation; erratic provincial purchasing policies; distribution of sales; and lack of professional mobility. In Europe, however, barriers to trade did not fall completely with the thrust towards 1 January 1993. Cabotage in both trucking and the airline industry is still a major constraint to the free passage of goods and people that was originally envisioned.

A quite different political precedent was created when John Brown Engineering (a British company) attempted to sell turbine engines to the then Soviet Union for use in its gas pipeline distribution system. The rotor blades were sub-licensed from General Electric, so when President Reagan vetoed all American sales of technology to the Soviet Union, this veto included products such as this which had a key American component in it. Mrs Thatcher, then British Prime Minister, threatened John Brown Engineering with repercussions in its home market if it did not supply, but it was being threatened equally with sanctions in the US market (which was important to the company) if it did comply with its own government's wishes: a most awkward situation in which to be placed. Negotiations resolved the issue and the British government won its point over the US Administration, but it sent shock waves through many boardrooms. Elsewhere, governments are able to enforce their trading requirements through the use of quotas (which are published) and 'desires' (which are not), but are implemented through the use of VERs (voluntary export restraints) which place a virtual quota on imports. Whereas these do not have any legal status, importers know that to exceed these stated quotas will bring down the wrath of the government on them. To this extent only, it is voluntary compliance which takes place.

Ten easy ways to lose your customer's trust

1. Produce poor quality products.
2. Do not worry about the corporate image.
3. Do not worry about customer service.
4. If you break Rule No. 3, cut corners or cost.
5. Do not communicate with customers.
6. If you make a mistake, do not admit it.
7. Do not be reliable.
8. Misrepresent your products.
9. Do not worry about high employee turnover and employee satisfaction.
10. Have 'creative' corporate policies.

Source: Earl Naumann (1992), 'Ten easy ways to lose your customer's trust', *Business Horizons*, September–October, pp. 30–3. Reprinted from *Business Horizons*, September–October 1992. Copyright © 1992 by the Foundation for the School of Business at Indiana University. Used with permission.

Similarly, no nation openly condones bribery. In the countries where we find something that we in the Western hemisphere may choose to call 'bribery', it is usually known by some inoffensive term in the local language. Also, and here is where politics enters in, every country seeks to give support to its exporters and some countries extend this very favourable tax treatment to exporters to allow for payment of foreign commissions on export sales. The word 'bribery' does not arise, but it is the other half of the same picture that we are seeing. Is bribery simply a question of degree? Is domestic legislation such as the US Foreign Corrupt Practices Act (FCPA) anything more than just something to settle the minds of American voters at home? As John L. Graham put it (1983), there are three basic questions:

1. The legal question: is the payment illegal under the FCPA and what are the consequences of getting caught?
2. The ethical question: is it right or wrong?
3. The economic question: is the payment really necessary? What happens if I say no?

All three will engender wide-ranging discussion from the morality of these payments to their effectiveness in relation to other forms of promotion or commission payments.

Legal

Legislation is almost by its very character anachronistic for the society that it serves to protect. Legislation is too often enacted to deal with yesterday's problems rather than tomorrow's potential conflicts. Most often it is simply a snapshot of how society viewed a social issue at a given point in time. As society changes, attitudes soften and become more liberal and so pressure groups form to liberalize the legal system further, whether it be a question of repression, self-expression, human rights or basic access to the system for legal redress.

In the international context, there is no actual body of law known as international law unless related to the law of the sea. International law more usually relates to incidents of domestic legislation, most commonly US legislation extending its territorial reach. North Sea oil only became a commercial reality once ownership of the oil and gas reserves had been established by an international conference on the law of the sea, partitioning ownership rights to the adjoining countries. Law had to be in place for investment to begin and for governments then to determine their tariff rates for petroleum excise duties.

While international law does not exist, what does often reconcile international disputes is the use of arbitration courts. These arbitration courts do not have full legal powers or recognition but their decisions have almost always been upheld whenever an arbitration ruling has subsequently been contested in open court. The arbitration council is usually either industry based or else international, as in the case of the Paris Chamber of Commerce which is an important player in the area of international arbitration and conflict resolution. The various arbitration councils come under the control of UNCITRAL (United Nations' Committee for International Trade Law) which has been slow to codify and formally recognize their importance.

Twelve most common mistakes of potential exporters

1. Failure to obtain qualified export counselling and to develop a master international marketing plan before starting an export business.
2. Insufficient commitment by top management to overcome the legal difficulties and financial requirements of exporting.
3. Insufficient care in selecting overseas distributors.
4. Chasing orders from around the world instead of establishing a basis for profitable operations and orderly growth.
5. Neglecting export business when the domestic market booms.
6. Failure to treat international distributors on an equal basis with domestic counterparts.
7. Assuming that a given market technique and product will automatically be successful in all countries.
8. Unwillingness to modify products to meet regulations or cultural preference of other countries.
9. Failure to print service, sale and warranty messages in locally understood languages.
10. Failure to consider use of an export management company.
11. Failure to consider licensing or joint venture agreements.
12. Failure to provide readily available servicing for the product.

Source: US Department of Commerce (1990), *A Basic Guide to Exporting*, NTC: Lincolnwood, IL.

Disputes may arise for reasons other than simply a dispute between two partners. Sometimes it involves one trading partner claiming that it cannot fulfil a contract because of an action taken by its government and so seeks refuge in a legal defence of *force majeure*, which means that, for reasons completely outside its control, it is unable to fulfil a supply contract into which it had voluntarily entered. Claims of *force majeure* are usually contested through the courts but the legal costs will be high and legal decisions are not obtained quickly, so an ongoing situation may totally disintegrate before any legal decision is reached. To this end, most companies will seek to avoid the fees and the lengthy duration of the legal process and opt instead for industrial arbitration, both sides agreeing that the decision taken will be binding on either side.

However, it is on national legal systems that these verdicts are based and there is no one particular legal system better suited to international trading activities than any other. Contracts will usually state that, in the event of dispute, the law of the named country will prevail. Overriding this, however, is the extraterritorial reach of the United States. Its export licensing and its Foreign Corrupt Practices Act are but two examples of ways in which its domestic legislation travels beyond its national frontiers. Sometimes the United States sorely tries the patience of its allies. Take the example of the following report:

> Two years ago, a US court gave a preliminary opinion that the market in which UK-produced North Sea Brent crude oil is bought, sold and delivered mainly in Europe – was a US futures market. Traders hardly batted an eyelid as they thought the position too absurd to be upheld. On April 18, however, the court's pronouncement was confirmed implying that traders may be in violation of US law, under which off-exchange futures transactions are illegal. ('Oil market in limbo', *The Financial Times*, London, 3 May 1990)

A new precedent was being created. It was not an isolated incident, as earlier, unitary taxation, a Californian invention, was introduced to tax the worldwide profits of multinationals based in the United States. Unitary taxation was much hated and hotly contested, but was introduced by many states and lasted for several years before being repealed.

Social

A country may comprise several nations and within each there may be several independent cultures and sub-cultures which divide up into religions or cults or just fashion-followers. From the outset it is useful to think in terms of three levels of constraint which have to be surmounted in order to achieve successful product penetration, especially if this product embodies a concept new to the nation-state that is the target market. At the first level there are habits and conventions which influence how people normally perform tasks. Mounting a challenge at this level, by illustrating how you can perform the same task more efficiently, particularly if at similar or lower cost, will result in success. First calculators took over from slide rules, then computers took over from cash registers. The silent revolution that took place was totally effective and met no opposition.

At the next level, however, there is what we may call 'mores', the Latin word for the morals and religion of the country concerned. To undertake any act that directly conflicts with the mores of the country is pure folly and doomed to failure. Product concepts should be screened so that at the earliest opportunity ill-advised plans to have, for example, wine bars in a Muslim country are killed off before they leave the drawing board. Similarly, naivety and ignorance of the culture may lead to totally inappropriate advertising that may be ambiguous, incomprehensible or even insulting. In the same way graphic design, colour and aesthetics change from one society to another. To take a concrete example, Electrolux, the Swedish company that sells vacuum cleaners as well as refrigerators and freezers, had an advertising campaign in the United Kingdom

---

Ten rules for a company in trouble

1. Make sure the real crisis is identified.
2. Power is what you have and what the opposition thinks you have.
3. Never go outside the experience of your people.
4. Go outside the opposition's experience.
5. Make the opposition play by their own rules.
6. Issues that drag on too long become drags themselves.
7. Keep the pressure on.
8. The threat is usually more terrifying than the problem itself.
9. You have nothing to lose and everything to gain.
10. The price of a successful attack is a constructive alternative.

Source: Geoffrey D. Lurie (1992), 'Ten rules for a company in trouble', *Business Horizons*, September–October, pp. 67–9. After Saul Alinsky's 'Rules for radicals', originally developed to be used against the corporate world. Reprinted from *Business Horizons*, September–October 1992. Copyright © 1992 by the Foundation for the School of Business at Indiana University. Used with permission.

that would bring a wry smile to an uncomprehending and confused American. Electrolux had a bold advertising campaign that simply showed a blown-up photograph of its vacuum cleaner and, below, the slogan 'Electrolux sucks!'. To a North American, this might as well say 'Electrolux is rubbish' – not quite the impact that was intended by their 'clever' advertising.

Benetton is another company that has aroused controversy over its international advertising campaign 'the colours of Benetton' which, in separate advertisements forming a campaign theme, seeks to shock by using visuals that include nuns, newborn babies and seagulls drowning in oil slicks.

Commercial

Precedents may be created in the way in which you treat your foreign customer in terms of pricing, for example. It has been established that it is cheaper to practise 'dumping' of excess supply in other foreign markets than to practise discounting to established customers, for once a discount is granted it is difficult to take it away. A precedent has been struck and a new expectation created.

Precedents may also be created in the treatment of foreign commission agents. How, for example, should one deal with the situation that may arise when a foreign customer approaches the head office direct with an order? Should the foreign agent then receive a commission to which they may feel legally entitled although in practice they have contributed nothing? The need to reward a good agent may justify a payment, but what if this particular agent is ineffectual?

Apart from payments there is also the question of foreign market pricing. There are few good precedents to follow, so even if a company is walking blindly into a market and pursuing only what may amount to a strategy by default, it is still creating precedents for itself. Price standardization internationally is difficult to achieve and open to a number of different forms of abuse, from transfer pricing to parallel trade and grey exports/imports. Pricing is dealt with in Chapter 6, but again provides a reminder of the way in which marketers have to answer to a number of different publics besides customers and that, when dealing with international markets, the number of these marketing publics effectively doubles. Apart from home and host governments, there are shareholders and existing and potential customers; also, internal marketing is required when changes have to be sold to the company workforce. Externally, too, there are financial publics, e.g. stockbrokers and analysts who scrutinize annual reports for possible intrinsic weaknesses, media publics who can be very important in promoting the firm generally and its innovations, citizen action publics who often fight a rearguard action in righting wrongs and injustices, local publics situated next to the company's head offices or plant, and the general public at large who may adopt a partisan attitude towards one of their companies being unfairly treated abroad. Plenty of examples of this are to be found in the 'Japan-bashing' that is going on in Europe and the United States. The public wants to buy national, but because of past experience with poor quality and indifferent attitudes, the buying public is turning towards the Japanese not as first choice, but as the only choice. Buying a car, for example, is one of the largest single expenditures the average individual will make. In terms of promotion all manufacturers are saying basically the same thing, but they vary in substance. Japanese auto manufacturers do not sell on price, whereas the American auto manufacturers do. Japanese auto manufacturers focus on value created for the customer; American manufacturers focus on price and include features found in their competitors' models. Once a precedent of this sort has been created, it is very difficult to break the cycle.

The message to the customer may focus on product quality, but why then is there a need to discount or offer rebates? The answer is a tradition that has been established and resultant customer expectations. The net effect is a confused, garbled message that lacks impact with the buying public. To be effective you have to focus the message you want to send to your buying public. It is not possible to send two conflicting messages simultaneously and expect to be successful. This has yet to be learned, however.

Checklist: be aware

1. Political intervention by home or host government.
2. Trading opportunities from the host country base.
3. Motivation for investing in a foreign market may be defensive or pre-emptive, as well as proactive.
4. Artificial trade restrictions and non-tariff barriers.
5. Political 'whipsawing'.

6. Taxation treatment of overseas commission payments.
7. Extant and pending legislation likely to materially affect the company and the sale of its products or services abroad.
8. International law does not exist as a body of law.
9. Extraterritoriality of domestic law, particularly US law.
10. Importance of arbitration in settling international disputes.
11. Tacit recognition of arbitration decisions by courts of law.
12. *Force majeure* as a legal loophole to escape the penalties for non-fulfilment of a supply contract.
13. In the host country, facilitating payments may be the norm to 'lubricate the administrative machinery'. In the home market this may be seen as bribery and corruption.
14. Cultural insensitivity or total unpreparedness will lead to the failure to recognize several important cultures or sub-cultures within the same nation-state.
15. Culture at the level of 'mores', meaning morals or religion, has to be respected in terms of how to approach the market.
16. Language, particularly the use of local language, may backfire and make the foreign product appear to be locally made, which in developing countries may carry significantly negative implications.
17. Consider how you treat your commission agents. Do they automatically receive commission on all sales from the market they serve, regardless of whether they were involved in those sales?
18. Dumping is illegal, but may be cheaper than offering discounts to clients in your home market.
19. The number of marketing publics doubles when you venture into international marketing.
20. Ingrown industries are the most vulnerable to foreign competition. An ingrown industry is essentially myopic and identifiable by managers making comments such as 'I have been in this industry for twenty years and know it like the back of my hand . . .'. Generally these industries fail to recognize the competitive threats of substitute products or possible new and foreign entrants to their markets before they are swamped by them.
21. Xenophobia is particularly prevalent when the serious competitors come from abroad. As Oscar Wilde put it: 'Nationalism is the last refuge of the scoundrel.' Currently it is reflected in 'Japan-bashing', but this is a sterile, negative activity that draws the focus away from the inability of domestic manufacturers to match their foreign competitors on the usual competitive criteria such as quality, reliability, etc., and focuses the search for solutions on trade protectionism.

References and further reading

Armstrong, Larry, Karen Lowny Miller and David Woodruff (1993), 'Toyota's new pickup: Oops', *Business Week*, 15 February, p. 37

Daily Telegraph (1988), *How to Export*, Daily Telegraph Business Enterprise Books: London

Davis, Edward W. (1992) 'Global outsourcing: Have US managers thrown the baby out with the bathwater?', *Business Horizons*, July–August, pp. 58–65

Fediman, Jeffrey A. (1986), 'A traveller's guide to gifts and bribes', *Harvard Business Review*, July–August, pp. 122–36

Graham, John L. A. (1983), 'Foreign corrupt practices: A manager's guide', *Columbia Journal of World Business*, Fall, pp. 89–94

Harbrecht, Douglas and Geri Smith (1993), 'A noose around NAFTA', *Business Week*, 22 February, p. 57

Kirpalani, V. H. (Manek) (1990), *International Business Handbook*, Haworth: New York

Lorinc, John (1993), 'Brawl in the family', *Canadian Business*, March, pp. 74–88

Lurie, Geoffrey D. (1992), 'Ten rules for a company in trouble', *Business Horizons*, September–October, pp. 67–9

Meyerovitz, Steven A. (1987), 'Treading the line between "grease" and bribery', *Business Marketing*, January, pp. 93–4

Naumann, Earl (1992), 'Ten easy ways to lose your customer's trust', *Business Horizons*, September–October, pp. 30–3

'Oil market in limbo', *The Financial Times*, 3 May 1990

Paliwoda, Stanley J. (1991), *New Perspectives on International Marketing*, Routledge: London

Tully, Shawn (1993), 'Can Boeing reinvent itself?', *Fortune*, 8 March, pp. 66–74

US Department of Commerce (1990), *A Basic Guide to Exporting*, NTC: Lincolnwood, IL

Bibliography

Books

Albaum, Gerald, Jesper Standskov, Edwin Duerr and Laurence Dowd (1989), *International Marketing and Export Management*, Addison-Wesley: Wokingham

Axtell, Roger E. (1989), *The Do's and Taboos of International Trade*, John Wiley: New York

Axtell, Roger E. (1990), *Do's and Taboos Around the World*, John Wiley: New York

Badaracco, Joseph L. (1991), *The Knowledge Link: How firms compete through strategic alliances*, Harvard Business School Press: Boston, MA

Baines, Adam (1992), *The Handbook of International Direct Marketing*, Kogan Page: London

Buckley, Peter J. and Pervez Ghauri (1993), *The Internationalisation of the Firm*, Harcourt Brace Jovanovich: London

Butler, Jack (1988), *The Importer's Handbook*, Woodhead-Faulkner: Cambridge

Buzzell, Robert D. and John A. Quelch (1988), *Multinational Marketing Management: Cases and readings*, Addison-Wesley: Reading, MA

Buzzell, Robert D., John A. Quelch and Christopher Bartlett (1992), *Global Marketing Management: Cases and readings*, 2nd edn, Addison-Wesley: Reading, MA

Cannon, Tom and Mike Willis (1986), *How to Buy and Sell Overseas*, Hutchinson: London

Cavusgil, S. Tamer and Pervez N. Ghauri (1990), *Doing Business in Developing Countries*, Routledge: London

Cavusgil, S. Tamer and Tiger Li (1992), *International Marketing: An annotated bibliography*, American Marketing Association: Chicago, IL

149

Christopher, Martin, Adam Payne and David Ballanbyne (1991), *Relationship Marketing: Bringing quality, customer service and marketing together*, Heinemann: Oxford

Crosby, Philip B. (1979), *Quality is Free*, McGraw-Hill: New York

Cundiff, Edward W. and Marye T. Hilger (1988), *Marketing in the International Environment*, 2nd edn, Prentice Hall: Englewood Cliffs, NJ

Czinkota, Michael R. and Ilkka A. Ronkainen (1990), *International Marketing*, Holt, Reinhart and Winston: Orlando, FL

Dahringer, Lee D. and Hans Muhlbacher (1991), *International Marketing: A global perspective*, Addison-Wesley: Reading, MA

Daily Telegraph (1988), *How to Export*, Daily Telegraph Business Enterprise Books: London

de Mooij, Marieke K. and Warren Keegan (1991), *Advertising Worldwide: Concepts, theories and practice of international, multinational and global advertising*, Prentice Hall: Hemel Hempstead

Department of Trade and Industry, *The Single Market: A guide to public purchasing*, London

de Rouffignac, Peter Danton (1991), *Europe's New Business Culture*, Pitman: London

Drucker, Peter F. (1989), *The New Realities*, Butterworth-Heinemann: Oxford

Forsgren, Mats and Jan Johanson (1992), *Managing Networks in International Business*, Gordon and Breach: Philadelphia

Goldstein, Steven M. (1991), *Mini Dragons: Hong Kong, Singapore, South Korea, Taiwan: Fragile economic markets in the Pacific*, Westview: San Francisco, CA

Harris, Philip R. and Robert T. Moran (1991), *Managing Cultural Differences*, 3rd edn, Gulf: Houston, TX

INCOTERMS 1990, publication no. 460, ICC: Paris, France

Jeannet, Jean-Pierre and Hubert D. Hennessey (1992), *Global Marketing Strategies*, 2nd edn, Houghton-Mifflin: Boston, MA

Jefkins, Frank (1987), *International Dictionary of Marketing and Communications*, Blackie: Glasgow and London

Kaynak, Erdener (1991), *Sociopolitical Aspects of International Marketing*, Haworth: New York

Kennedy, Gavin (1984), *Everything is Negotiable!*, Hutchinson: London

Kirpalani, V. H. (Manek) (1990), *International Business Handbook*, Haworth: New York

Levitt, Theodore (1983), *The Marketing Imagination*, Macmillan: New York

Livingstone, J. M. (1989), *The Internationalisation of Business*, Macmillan: Basingstoke

Maslow, A. H. (1954), *Motivation and Personality*, Harper and Brothers: New York

Morris, Mag (1985), *Importing for the Small Business*, Kogan Page: London

Nelson, Carl A. (1990), *Import/Export: How to get started in international trade*, Liberty Hall Press: Blue Ridge Summit, PA

Nohria, Nitin and Robert G. Eccles (1992), *Networks and Organisations: Structure, form and action*, Harvard Business School Press: Boston, MA

Ohmae, Kenichi (1985), *Triad Power: The coming shape of global competition*, Collier Macmillan: London

Ohmae, Kenichi (1990), *The Borderless World: Power and strategy in the interlinked economy*, HarperCollins: New York

Paliwoda, Stanley J. (1989), 'Countertrade', in Michael J. Thomas (ed.), *The Marketing Handbook*, 3rd edn, Gower Press: Aldershot

Paliwoda, Stanley J. (1991), *New Perspectives on International Marketing*, Routledge: London

Paliwoda, Stanley J. (1993), *International Marketing*, 2nd edn, Butterworth-Heinemann: Oxford

Peters, Thomas J. and Robert H. Waterman (1982), *In Search of Excellence: Lessons from America's best-run companies*, Fitzhenry and Whiteside: New York

Porter, Michael E. (1990), *The Competitive Advantage of Nations*, Macmillan: London

Ryans, John K. Jr and Pradeep A. Rau (1990), *Marketing Strategies for the New Europe: A North American perspective on 1992*, American Marketing Association: Chicago, IL

Sherlock, Paul (1991), *Rethinking Business to Business Marketing*, Macmillan: New York

Smith, A. E., J. M. MacLachlan, W. Lazer and P. La Barbera (1989), *Marketing 2000 – Future Perspectives on Marketing: An annotated bibliography of articles*, American Marketing Association: Chicago, IL

Stock, James R. and Douglas M. Lambert (1987), *Strategic Logistics Management*, 2nd edn, Richard D. Irwin: Homewood, IL, p. 42

Toop, Alan (1992), *European Sales Promotion: Great campaigns in action*, Kogan Page: London

Turnbull, Peter W. and Stanley J. Paliwoda (1986), *Research in International Marketing*, Croom-Helm: London

Turnbull, Peter W. and Jean-Paul Valla (1986), *Strategies for International Industrial Marketing*, Croom-Helm: London

US Department of Commerce (1990), *A Basic Guide to Exporting*, NTC: Lincolnwood, IL

Valentine, Charles F. (1990), *The Arthur Young International Business Guide*, John Wiley: New York

Vardar, Nukhet (1992), *Global Advertising: Rhyme or reason?*, Paul Chapman: London

Wells, L. Fargo and Kevin B. Dulat (1990), *Exporting from Start to Finance*, Liberty Hall Press: Blue Ridge Summit, PA

Articles

Adamson, Colin (1993), 'Evolving complaint procedures', *Managing Service Quality*, **3** (2), pp. 439–44

Alexander, Nicholas (1990), 'Retailers and international markets: Motives or expansion?', *International Marketing Review*, 7 (4), pp. 75–85

Allen, Kathleen M. (1991), 'The role of logistics in the overseas plant selection decision process of United States-based multinational corporations', *Journal of Business Logistics*, 12 (2), pp. 59–72

'Anatomy of costly, false rumour', *Globe and Mail*, Toronto, 2 July 1991, pp. A1, A15

Armstrong, Larry, Karen Lowny Miller and David Woodruff (1993), 'Toyota's new pickup: Oops', *Business Week*, 15 February, p. 37

Belli, Pedro (1991), 'Globalising the rest of the world', *Harvard Business Review*, July–August, pp. 50–5

Blenkhorn, David L. and Peter M. Banting (1991), 'How reverse marketing changes buyer–seller roles', *Industrial Marketing Management*, 20, p. 189

Boddewyn, Jean J. (1992), 'Fitting socially in Fortress Europe: Understanding, reaching, and impressing Europeans', *Business Horizons*, November–December, pp. 35–44

Britt, Stuart Henderson (1969), 'Are so-called successful advertising campaigns really successful?', *Journal of Advertising Research*, 9, June, pp. 3–9

Brockhouse, Gordon (1992), 'A phone call that does it all', *Canadian Business*, December, pp. 98–103

Brown, Donna (1990), 'Game-winning strategies for Europe's new market', *Management Review*, May, pp. 10–15

Byrne, Patrick (1992), 'Logistics in Europe: Success will require radical changes', *Transportation and Distribution*, October, pp. 60–3

Camp, Robert C. (1992), 'Learning from the best leads to superior performance', *Journal of Business Strategy*, 13 (1), pp. 3–6

Carruthers, John C. (1984), 'Technology-driven and market-driven life cycles: Implications for multinational corporate strategy', *Columbia Journal of World Business*, Summer, pp. 56–60

Caulkin, Simon (1990), 'Last of the ad-venturers', *Management Today*, February, pp. 54–8

'Celestial Seasonings/Perrier to market ready-to-drink tea', *Marketing News*, American Marketing Association, Chicago, 17 February 1992

Cerruti, James L. and Joseph Holtzman (1990), 'Business strategy in the new European landscape', *Journal of Business Strategy*, November–December, p. 22

Chan, Allan K. K. (1990), 'Localisation in international branding: A preliminary investigation on Chinese names of foreign brands in Hong Kong', *International Journal of Advertising*, 9, pp. 81–91

'Clout! More and more, retail giants rule the marketplace', *Business Week*, 21 December 1992, pp. 66–73

Crainer, Stuart (1990), 'Putting strategy to work', *Marketing Business*, December, pp. 20–1

Czinkota, Michael R. and Ilkka A. Ronkainen (1992), 'Global marketing 2000: A marketing survival guide', *Marketing Management*, 1 (1), pp. 36–45

Davis, Edward W. (1992), 'Global outsourcing: Have US managers thrown the baby out with the bathwater?', *Business Horizons*, July–August, pp. 58–65

Department of Trade and Industry (1993), *The Single Market: A guide to public purchasing*, London

Douglas, Susan P. and C. Samuel Craig (1989), 'Evolution of global marketing strategy: Scale, scope and synergy', *Columbia Journal of World Business*, Fall, pp. 47–59

Douglas, Susan P. and Yoram Wind (1987), 'The myth of globalisation', *Columbia Journal of World Business*, Winter, pp. 19–29

Doz, Y. L. and C. K. Prahalad (1991), 'Managing DMNC's: A search for a new paradigm', *Strategic Management Journal*, **12**, pp. 145–64

Ellram, Lisa M. (1992), 'Patterns in international alliances', *Journal of Business Logistics*, **13** (1), pp. 1–25

Fagan, Mark L. (1991), 'A guide to global sourcing', *Journal of Business Strategy*, March–April, pp. 21–5

Fediman, Jeffrey A. (1986), 'A traveller's guide to gifts and bribes', *Harvard Business Review*, July–August, pp. 122–36

Flint, Jerry (1993), 'The myth of U.S. manufacturing's decline', *Forbes*, 18 January, pp. 40–2

Forsgren, Mats, Ulf Holm and Jan Johanson (1990), 'Internationalisation of the second degree', paper presented to the Academy of International Business UK Regional Conference, University of Strathclyde, Glasgow, 6–7 April

Fuhrman, Peter (1992), 'Getting in bed together', *Forbes*, 11 May, pp. 86–7

Garda, Robert A. (1992), 'Tactical pricing', *McKinsey Quarterly*, **3**, pp. 75–85

'The global economy: Who gets hurt?', *Business Week*, 10 August 1992, pp. 48–53

Godiwalla, Yezdi H. (1986), 'Multinational planning: Developing a global approach', *Long Range Planning*, **19** (2), pp. 110–16

Graham, John L. A. (1983), 'Foreign corrupt practices: A manager's guide', *Columbia Journal of World Business*, Fall, pp. 89–94

Haley, Russell J. (1963), 'Benefit segmentation: A decision oriented research tool', *Journal of Marketing*, July, pp. 30–5

Hamel, Gary and C. K. Prahalad (1985), 'Do you really have a global strategy?', *Harvard Business Review*, July–August, pp. 139–48

Hamel, Gary and C. K. Prahalad (1989), 'Strategic intent', *Harvard Business Review*, May–June, pp. 63–76

Harbrecht, Douglas and Geri Smith (1993), 'A noose around NAFTA', *Business Week*, 22 February, p. 57

Helper, Donald G. and H. Chang Moon (1990), 'Striving for first-rate markets in Third World nations', *Management Review*, May, pp. 20–2

Herbert, Ira C. (1988), 'How Coke markets to the world', *Journal of Business Strategy*, September–October, pp. 4–7

Higgins, S. and J. Ryans (1991), 'EC-1992 and international advertising agencies', *International Journal of Advertising*, **10** (4), pp. 293–8

Hirschhorn, Larry and Thomas Gilmore (1992), 'The new boundaries of the "boundaryless" corporation', *Harvard Business Review*, May–June, pp. 104–15

Hisatomi, Takashi (1991), 'Global marketing by the Nissan Motor Co. Ltd', *Marketing and Research Today*, **19** (1), pp. 56–62

Howard, D. G. and M. A. Mayo (1988), 'Developing a defensive product management philosophy for Third World markets', *International Marketing Review*, **5** (1), pp. 31–40

Howells, Robert (1991), 'How to price products competitively in Europe', *Target Marketing*, **14** (5), pp. 32–4

Hurst, Stephen (1993), 'Revealed at source', *Managing Service Quality*, **3** (2), pp. 449–52

Jain, Subhash C. (1989), 'Standardisation of international marketing strategy: Some research hypotheses', *Journal of Marketing*, **53**, January, pp. 70–9

Joelson, Mark R. and Roger C. Wilson (1992), 'An international dumping primer: Know the rules before an antidumping complaint arrives', *Journal of European Business*, **3** (4), pp. 53–5, 64

Johanson, Jan and Jan-Erik Vahlne (1990), 'The mechanism of internationalisation', *International Marketing Review*, **7** (4), pp. 11–24

Jones, Robert E., L. W. Jacobs and W. Van't Spijker (1992), 'Strategic decision processes in international firms', *Management International Review*, **32** (3), pp. 219–36

Kanso, Ali (1991), 'The use of advertising agencies for foreign markets: Decentralised decisions and localised approaches?', *International Journal of Advertising*, **10** (2), pp. 129–36

Karel, Jan-Willum (1991), 'Brand strategy positions products worldwide', *Journal of Business Strategy*, May–June, pp. 16–19

Kartbech-Olesen, Ruby (1989), 'World trade in cephalopods: A growing business', *International Trade Forum*, **25** (2), pp. 4–7, 30

Kashani, Kamran (1989), 'Beware the pitfalls of global marketing', *Harvard Business Review*, September–October, pp. 91–8

Kashani, Kamran and John A. Quelch (1990), 'Can sales promotion go global?', *Business Horizons*, May–June, pp. 37–43

Keegan, Warren J., Richard R. Still and John J. Hill (1987), 'Transferability and adaptability of products and promotion themes in multinational marketing: MNC's in LDC's', *Journal of Global Marketing*, **1** (1/2), Fall/Winter, pp. 85–103

Killough, James (1978), 'Improved pay-offs from transnational advertising', *Harvard Business Review*, July–August, pp. 102–10

Klein, Saul and Victor J. Roth (1993), 'Satisfaction with international marketing channels', *Journal of the Academy of Marketing Science*, **21** (1), pp. 39–44

Knetter, Michael M. (1989), 'Price discrimination by U.S. and German exporters', *American Economic Review*, **79** (1), pp. 198–210

Koepfler, Edward R. (1989), 'Strategic options for global market players', *Journal of Business Strategy*, July–August, pp. 46–50

Kosaka, Hiroshi (1992), 'A global marketing strategy responding to national cultures', *Marketing and Research Today*, **20** (4), pp. 245–56

Kotler, Philip (1986), 'Megamarketing', *Harvard Business Review*, **64** (2), pp. 117–25

Kublin, Michael (1990), 'A guide to export pricing', *Industrial Management*, **32** (3), pp. 29–32

Lee, Chong S. and Yoo S. Yang (1990), 'Impact of export market expansion strategy on export performance', *International Marketing Review*, **7** (4), pp. 41–51

Lennon, Judie (1991), 'Developing brand strategies across borders', *Marketing and Research Today*, **19** (3), pp. 160–9

Leontiades, Jim (1990), 'Market share and corporate strategy in international industries', *Journal of Business Strategy*, **5** (1), pp. 30–7

Leszinski, Rolf (1992), 'Pricing for a single market', *McKinsey Quarterly*, **3**, pp. 86–94

Levitt, Theodore (1960), 'Marketing myopia', *Harvard Business Review*, July–August, pp. 45–56

Levitt, Theodore (1983), 'After the sale is over', *Harvard Business Review*, September–October, pp. 87–93

Levy, Brigitte (1992), 'NAFTA: The competitiveness challenge', *Dimensions of International Business*, **8**, School of Business, Carleton University International Business Study Group, Ottawa, Canada, Fall, p. 45

Levy, Matthew D. and Soji Teramura (1993), 'Foreign ownership: Study offers Japanese on new agenda', *Management Review*, January, pp. 49–54

Lorinc, John (1993), 'Brawl in the family', *Canadian Business*, March, pp. 74–88

Lurie, Geoffrey D. (1992), 'Ten rules for a company in trouble', *Business Horizons*, September–October, pp. 67–9

Main, Jeremy (1989), 'How to go global – and why', *Fortune*, 28 August, pp. 70–6

Meyerovitz, Steven A. (1987), 'Treading the line between "grease" and bribery', *Business Marketing*, January, pp. 93–4

Moody, Patricia E. (1992), 'Customer supplier integration: Why being an excellent customer counts', *Business Horizons*, July–August, pp. 52–7

Moore, Richard A. (1991), 'Relationship states in an international marketing channel', *European Journal of Marketing*, **25** (5), pp. 47–59

Morais, Richard C. (1993), 'Patently absurd', *Forbes*, 18 January, p. 46

Morita, Akio (1992), 'Partnering for competitiveness: The role of Japanese business', *Harvard Business Review*, May–June, pp. 76–83

Mueller, Barbara (1991), 'An analysis of information content in standardised vs specialised multinational advertisements', *Journal of International Business Studies*, **22** (1), pp. 23–39

Murphy, Paul R., Douglas R. Dalenberg and James M. Daley (1991), 'Analysing international water transportation: The perspectives of large U.S. industrial corporations', *Journal of Business Logistics*, **12** (1), pp. 169–90

Murphy, Paul R., James M. Daley and Douglas R. Dalenberg (1991a),

'Forwarders are a vital link for shippers', *Transportation and Distribution*, August, p. 44

Murphy, Paul R., James M. Daley and Douglas R. Dalenberg (1991b), 'Smaller shippers play important global role', *Transportation and Distribution*, December, pp. 41–9

Naumann, Earl (1992), 'Ten easy ways to lose your customer's trust', *Business Horizons*, September–October, pp. 30–3

Norton, Rob (1993), 'Will tough talk mean trade wars?', *Fortune*, **127** (5), pp. 93–7

'Oil market in limbo', *The Financial Times*, 3 May 1990

Onkvisit, Sak and John J. Shaw (1988), 'Marketing barriers in international trade', *Business Horizons*, May–June, pp. 64–72

Palia, Aspy P. (1990), 'Worldwide network of countertrade services', *Industrial Marketing Management*, **19**, pp. 69–76

Paltschik, Mikael and Kaj Storbacka (1992), 'Monitoring the customer base to achieve profitability', *Marketing and Research Today*, **20** (3), pp. 155–67

Papadopoulos, N., L. A. Heslop and G. Bamossy (1989), 'International competitiveness of American and Japanese products', *Dimensions of International Business*, **2**, School of Business, Carleton University International Business Study Group, Ottawa

Parkinson, Stephen (1991), 'World class marketing: From lost empires to the image men', *Journal of Marketing Management*, **7**, pp. 299–311

Particelli, Marc C. (1990), 'A global arena', *Journal of Consumer Marketing*, **7** (4), Fall, pp. 43–52

Rafferty, James (1987), 'Exit barriers and strategic position in declining markets', *Long Range Planning*, **20** (2), pp. 86–91

Ramsbotham, General Sir David (1993), 'Marching as to work', *Professional Manager*, March, pp. 10–12

Ramunajam, V. and N. Venkatraman (1988), 'Excellence, planning and performance', *Interfaces*, May–June, pp. 23–31

Rau, Jane (1992), 'A gift for publicity', *Asian Business*, **28** (4), pp. 48–9

'The report on international commerce in Florida, the Southeast and the Americas', *International Business Chronicle*, Miami, Florida, 14–27 October 1991, p. 2

Rice, Faye (1992), 'What intelligent consumers want', *Fortune*, 28 December, pp. 56–60

Richardson, Helen L. A. (1991), 'Moving toward global safety', *Transportation and Distribution*, November, pp. 29–33

Robert, Michel H. (1990), 'Managing your company's strategy', *Journal of Business Strategy*, March–April, pp. 24–8

Roberts, Alan (1988), 'Setting export prices to sell competitively', *International Trade Forum*, **24** (3), pp. 10–13, 30–1

Rozon, Bernie (1991), 'Managing a worldwide logistics network', *Materials Management and Distribution*, July, pp. 15–18

Rutigliano, Anthony J. (1986), 'The debate goes on: Global vs local advertising', *Management Review*, **75** (6), pp. 27–31

Ryans, John K. Jr and David G. Ratz (1987), 'Advertising standardisation', *International Journal of Advertising*, **6**, pp. 145–58

Samiee, Saeed and Kendall Roth (1992), 'The influence of global marketing standardisation on performance', *Journal of Marketing*, **56** (2), pp. 1–17

Schmitz, Robert A. and Marc L. Rovner (1992), 'A world of diminishing distance: How information technology is collapsing the transaction barriers between marketers and consumers', *Marketing and Research Today*, **20** (4), pp. 227–36

Schonberger, Richard J. (1992), 'Is strategy strategic? Impact of total quality management on strategy', *Academy of Management Executive*, **6** (3), pp. 80–7

Schwoerer, Juergen (1987), 'Measuring advertising effectiveness: Emergence of an international standard?', *European Research*, **15** (1), pp. 40–51

Semple, Jack (1992), 'A pan-Europe problem', *Management Today*, June, pp. 101–2

Sherlock, Paul (1992), 'The irrationality of "rational" business buying decisions', *Marketing Management*, **1** (2), Spring, pp. 9–15

Sheth, Jagdish N. (1977), 'A market-oriented strategy of long-range planning for multinational corporations', *European Research*, January, pp. 3–12

Sims, C., A. Phillips and T. Richards (1992), 'Developing a global pricing strategy', *Marketing and Research Today*, **20** (1), pp. 3–15

Sokol, Reuben (1992), 'Gaining a world class edge', *CMA Magazine*, September, p. 17

Specks, Christine and Sundeep Sahay (1991), 'Segmentation of international markets for the remote sensing industry', *Dimensions of International Business*, **5**, Carleton University International Business Study Group, Ottawa, Spring, pp. 55–67

Sprout, Alison L. (1992), 'Products of the years', *Fortune*, 28 December, pp. 64–9

Srivam, V. and P. Gopalakrishna (1991), 'Can advertising be standardised among similar countries? A cluster-based analysis', *International Journal of Advertising*, **10** (2), pp. 137–49

Starr, Martin K. (1984), 'Global production and operations strategy', *Columbia Journal of World Business*, Winter, pp. 17–22

Stewart, Michael J. (1992), 'Tobacco consumption and advertising restrictions', *International Journal of Advertising*, **11** (2), pp. 97–118

Stewart, Thomas A. (1992), 'Brace for Japan's hot new strategy', *Fortune*, **126** (6), pp. 62–74

Strauss, M. (1992), 'Cashing in on the clear Canadian image', *Globe and Mail*, Toronto, 13 March

Studemann, Frederick (1992), 'Serious about Skoda', *International Management*, March, pp. 46–9

Taylor, William (1991), 'The logic of global business: An interview with ABB's Percy Barnevik', *Harvard Business Review*, March–April, pp. 91–105

'That's upbeat not beat-up', *Business Week*, 21 December 1992, p. 40

Trunick, Perry A. (1992a), 'British transportation goes commercial', *Trans-*

portation and Distribution, April, pp. 49–54

Trunick, Perry A. (1992b), 'Europe: A single market with complex logistics', Transportation and Distribution, October, pp. 51–63

Tully, Shawn (1993), 'Can Boeing reinvent itself?', Fortune, 8 March, pp. 66–74

'Value marketing: Quality, service and fair pricing are the keys to selling in the 90's', Business Week, 11 November 1991, pp. 132–7

Vandermerwe, Sandra and Marc-André L'Huellier (1989), 'Euro-consumers in 1992', Business Horizons, January–February, p. 39

Vardar, N. and S. Paliwoda (1993), 'Successful international advertising campaign and the "mirroring effect" between MNCs and their agencies', Journal of Euromarketing, 2 (4), pp. 45–66

Walters, Peter G. P. and Brian Toyne (1989), 'Product modification and standardisation in international markets: Strategic options and facilitating policies', Columbia Journal of World Business, Winter, pp. 37–44

Waterson, M. (1992), 'International advertising statistics', International Journal of Advertising, 11, pp. 14–68

Webb, Victor (1991), 'Media and cultural diversity in the Gulf countries', Middle East Executive Reports, 14 (5), pp. 10–12

Webster, Joel C. (1991), 'Technique surpasses standard quadrant analysis', Marketing News, 2 September, pp. 8–9

Welch, Lawrence S. (1992), 'Developments in international franchising', Journal of Global Marketing, 6 (1/2), pp. 81–97

Welch, Mary (1993), 'Database marketing explodes', Business Marketing, March, pp. 48–80

'When the state picks winners', The Economist, 9 January 1993, pp. 13–14

'Why Brussels sprouts', The Economist, 26 December 1992, pp. 70–2

Wikstrom, Solveig (1993), 'The customer as co-producer', Studies in Action and Enterprise, Department of Business Administration, Stockholm University, p. 1993:1

Witcher, Barry J. (1990), 'A new kind of marketing for Europe', Durham University Business School, Occasional Paper Series no. 9064

Wortzel, Lawrence H. and Heidi Vernon Wortzel (1981), 'Export marketing strategies for NIC and LDC-based firms', Columbia Journal of World Business, Spring, pp. 51–60

Yavas, Ugur, B. J. Verhage and R. T. Green (1992), 'Global consumer segmentation versus local market orientation: Empirical findings', Management International Review, 32 (3), pp. 265–72

Yip, George S. (1989), 'Global strategy: In a world of nations?', Sloan Management Review, 31, Fall, pp. 29–41

Young, Stephen (1990), 'Internationalisation: Introduction and overview', International Marketing Review, 7 (4), pp. 1–8

Index